# ONE GLORIOUS CHAIN

Three Welsh evangelists, their wives and friends who brought
Wales back to God in the eighteenth century revival.

A Glorious Chain of dynamic events.

## Christopher J. Tokeley

ARTHUR H. STOCKWELL LTD
Torrs Park, Ilfracombe, Devon, EX34 8BA
*Established 1898*
*www.ahstockwell.co.uk*

ISBN 978-0-7223-5061-4
*Printed in Great Britain by*
*Arthur H. Stockwell Ltd*
*Torrs Park   Ilfracombe*
*Devon  EX34 8BA*

# PICTURE CREDITS

# OTHER WORKS BY
# CHRISTOPHER J. TOKELEY

*Adam Ate with Dinosaurs*: *The Theory of Evolution: How It Came into Prominence, Why It Continues to Influence Our Thinking and What the Bible Teaches About Origins*, Athena Press, Twickenham, 2010. Obtainable from Amazon.

The author is also a contributor to http://www:wasdar.winright.com.

# ACKNOWLEDGMENTS

My thanks to my dear wife Brenda who corrected my spelling mistakes and grammar and made helpful suggestions and our family for their keen interest in this project.

I would like to thank staff at the National Library of Wales; Reverend Steve Brady, Editor "In Writing" and Steve Taylor, Librarian at the Evangelical Library, London. Hero von Frisen and Thomas Lloyd of the Philipps Family of Picton. The Picton Castle Trustees. The Carmarthenshire Museums Service. Reverend Richard Harrison, Baptist Minister of Pontypool for his reading the early stages of the book and his great encouragement to continue my research. Professor Julian Evans OBE., a descendant of Thomas and Sally Charles of Bala, for his reading of the manuscript and his helpful advice.

# CONTENTS

# ABOUT THE AUTHOR....

The author was born in London. He studied theology under Reverend Dr Ernest Kevan, BD, MTh, PhD, Principal of the London Bible College, (now London School of Theology), while continuing his career in international trade finance. He first heard about the eighteenth century revivals from his tutor at college, this led him to join the Evangelical Library for more research. In 1975 he was invited to lead the London Banks' Christian Union which he did until his retirement from the City of London in 1989. He edited the history of this old established charity for it's centenary before the documents were deposited in the Metropolitan Archives. Since then he has written articles for newspapers and magazines.

He is an occasional preacher in the Parish of Cove, Hampshire where he leads a men's group. He has contributed material for the website Was Darwin Right?

He is married with three grown children and six grandchildren.

# PREFACE

For some years I have observed from conversations with many people that few know about the longest and most dramatic years of revival of the Church in Wales. Most have heard of the 1904 Revival. Alas, few know about the period from about 1730 through to the early years of the nineteenth century. It is a sad state of affairs when Christian people in the principality and elsewhere have not heard of any of the men mentioned in this book, and under God's hand what monumental achievements were possible in the days before any modern technology, even before there were good roads. Therefore I believe there is a need to write a short and uncomplicated account of these men, together with their wives and companions, whom God used to preach the gospel to their countrymen in Wales during this period. Some lost their lives for the sake of the Kingdom of God.

The history of the Church in Wales in the eighteenth century fills one with awe because of the vigour and energetic zeal with which the gospel of our Lord Jesus Christ was proclaimed. From the third decade of the eighteenth century, well into the nineteenth century, revival ebbed and flowed in the Church in Wales. This was a gracious work of God. Some have described revival in the Church as like the tide – sometimes high, sometimes low, with its great surges and storms – or like a river when it is in full spate, carrying all before it with tremendous force and power. The work of God in reviving His Church cannot be contained within congregations as it brings change for good into the community in which the body of Christ is set as a witness. God's sovereignty is shown in revival; He may limit this gracious work to a town, a country or an ethnic group. He sends His blessing as He chooses. Sadly the work of the Holy Spirit may be opposed by obstinate resistance with disastrous results.

From reading Church history I know of no country other than Wales that has seen such a long period when religious fervour was sustained at its height; such times can only be ascribed to the powerful work of the Holy Spirit. Revival – or *diwygiad*, as the Welsh call this phenomenon – came to Llangeitho in 1730, and reached its zenith there in 1762, known as the Great Revival; then in Bala in 1791; then again there in 1817; in 1840 in Merioneth; then revival was centred on Anglesey and Caernavon in 1848 followed by the Second Evangelical Awakening, which spread from North America to the United Kingdom in 1859. Only the first three occurred in the years covered by this book. A young Christian, Sarah Jones, wrote to a friend in 1780 about the revival that was being experienced in South Wales, so this work of the Holy Spirit occurred with great power at other times and at various places in the principality.

All three of my Welsh 'heroes', as I affectionately call them, were ordained ministers of the Church of England. One was a minister for fifty-three years and made the Welsh the most literate people in Europe; the second had his licence to preach withdrawn because he was considered a Methodist, and seen mistakenly as a threat to the Established Church; the third was ordained, but was never able to find a permanent living in his homeland of Wales. He too was suspected of being a Methodist. For four years he was a curate in parishes in Somerset until love for a young lady caused him eventually to break with the Church of England after returning to Wales and finding no parish would engage him. When we read history books we seldom hear of great events being brought about by a man and woman who love one another. In the eighteenth century it happened! Some of their love letters in this book show the peculiarities of courtship of that time. So I have tried to make this book exciting, not a boring and dry history. I hope this and other anecdotes make the main characters and revival theme of the book come alive for you. The saving of souls was the passion of their lives.

One author wrote this about my heroes:

> They depicted sin in its enormity and they preached Christ crucified in all the fullness of his redeeming power. They were intensely and uncompromisingly dogmatic. They preached positive truth and waited for the blessing of the Holy Spirit, and they did not wait in vain. There is a continuity of privilege and blessing; there is nothing comparable to that of reverting to simple strong faith which inspired and sustained these apostolic men, who deemed the glory of God in the salvation of souls to be the primary and paramount object of the existence and organisation of the Church.

That was written over 100 years ago and still is appropriate to the Church in Wales, as it is to the rest of the United Kingdom.

It has been my aim to make this an enjoyable read for those who would not normally turn to history or biography, and also an exciting account of the work of three great men who were moved by God to promote the Kingdom of our Lord Jesus Christ. Each one was a link in a chain of events. I have tried through my research to find the true Christian character of these men and, where possible, their wives and what spurred them on to do the great work that brought a blessing to Wales and throughout the world. As I have researched them I have tried to draw alongside them and imagine what it was like to live in those times. These men were spiritual giants. It has been a great encouragement and blessing to me and my walk with the Lord. I hope you too will be blessed by reading this book and it will create a strong desire to experience the reviving power of the Holy Spirit in the Church.

There are a few matters to understand before the book is read. The word Methodist was a nickname for men and women who had come to a personal knowledge of Jesus Christ as their Lord and Saviour, and went about telling others of the gospel, very much like the early believers who earned the nickname 'Christian'. The Methodists did not separate themselves en bloc and become a separate denomination until early in the nineteenth century, after the period covered by this book. Furthermore, the reader must understand that the Established Church in Wales was the Church of England. The separation of the dioceses in Wales took place in 1920 and is now called the Church in Wales, with its own archbishop. The Bible texts quoted in the narrative were quoted from the Welsh Bible and subsequently translated into English. The texts below chapter headings and in Chapter 23 are taken from the New King James Version (NKJV).

Reliance has been on authors whose research was done by interviewing witnesses who knew these men and who had access to original documents. There are purposely few notes to interrupt the attention of the reader. If there were more, they would be from sources that are not easy to access. Some of the books used in my research are over 200 years old, and were borrowed from the Evangelical Library at Bounds Green, London. The different ways Welsh place names have been spelt over the centuries is very confusing, so I have kept to those you will find on current Ordnance Survey maps today. As to the names of Welsh people, I have kept to the modern spellings. This book is not written for academics (although they should read it); therefore I have not dwelt on the theological differences between George Whitefield and his Welsh friends and John Wesley.

Why read a book on Church history, or for that matter biography? I believe that unless we learn about some of the great movements brought about by the Holy Spirit we cannot pray with understanding for the situation that has arisen today in our own land with declining congregations. One former archbishop has put doubt into the minds of Anglicans about whether the Church of England will still be with us in a generation. So believers need to read this book and they may discover the way forward, if they are up to the challenge! Even the Bible tells us occasionally to look back:

> 'He has made His wonderful works
> to be remembered;
> The Lord is gracious and full of compassion.'
> Psalm 111:4

'Which we have heard and known,
And our fathers have told us.
We will not hide them from their children,
Telling to the generation to come
    the praises of the Lord.
And His strength and His
    wonderful works that He has done.'

Psalm 78:3–4

The children of Israel at every Passover celebrated what had happened in Egypt. The children recited the events that released them and their parents from a cruel regime in Egypt. Every time we receive the bread and wine at Holy Communion we remember what the Lord Jesus Christ did for us on the Cross, but also we can look forward to His coming in glory. When our children ask us what is the story behind the bread and wine we should tell how God delivered us from sin and hell and made our salvation secure in Christ Jesus. So reading about the work of the Holy Spirit should spur us on to pray for God's blessing on the Church today because we know the wonders God performed in the past and the greatness of His power. Surely He has power to re-energise the Church again, although He may not choose to do it in the same manner as in the eighteenth century. He will always honour the biblical exposition of His word and energise the Church through teaching that brings glory to His name. It should stir us to an energetic prayer life. Today the Church in the West is in the doldrums and it needs renewal to empower it to fulfil the commission that Jesus gave His disciples. When the Church is in decline it is always the prayer meeting that is lost from the Church notice sheet first.

The word 'revival' is mentioned often in this book and it must be understood what we mean by this often misused word. We must understand what the nature of true revival is. It is not to be confused with evangelism. It is not large meetings like the Billy Graham Crusades in London in the 1950s, although there were large meetings in the eighteenth century. We all thank God for the Crusades in the 1950s that brought thousands to know

Jesus Christ through evangelism. When God revives the Church that bears His name, the work He does begins in the Church but cannot be contained within it; the blessing overflows, bringing a very real presence of God not only to the Church, but also to society – that is revival. Church and society are changed! That is what the power of the gospel achieves in times of true Holy Spirit-breathed revival. That is what we need today – a movement of the Holy Spirit that empowers the Church, converts souls and brings change that reflects God's holiness in the morals of the Church and society.

The Reverend Duncan Campbell, a United Free Church Continuing minister and principal of the Faith Mission Bible College, often spoke about the revival that permeated the Church in the Western Isles of Scotland in the 1940s and '50s.[1] He described the change that the Holy Spirit brought about through the Church 'as God taking the field . . . sweeping the power of hell before the risen Christ, that is revival'. He recounted how 'A God *created hunger* brought people from their homes, work and dance halls, to hear the gospel.' I can still hear his broad Highland accent ringing in my ears as he told of events with passion that moved his listeners to prayer. People were moved to repent and put their faith in the risen Christ. He went on to tell how people were so deeply affected that crime and overindulgence in alcohol were swept away. Much the same happened in Wales during the times covered in this book.

Speaking to a crowded Keswick Convention in 1955,[2] the Reverend A. W. Rainsbury spoke passionately about the need for revival. I remember him defining revival as "Revival *is* an awareness of God. For it is in consciousness of that divine Presence that men see themselves for what they are, are broken down before Him, and in that breaking down are simultaneously revived by the grace of God."

The sermons of my heroes are available today and some have been edited and translated from Welsh into modern English. They are biblical and were challenging to their hearers at the time. It was God who used their words to bring people under powerful conviction of sin and the blessed hope that is in Christ. There are also similarities in the underlying attitudes of the public towards the gospel today, as there were in the eighteenth century, and these need to change as they did then. To enable this change to take place the Church needs to be first empowered by the Holy Spirit. All believers are part of the spiritual building we call the Church, so it is important we all know about the work of God in revival. Because the work of revival is wrought by God in people, it must become a very personal matter to each of us, as it did in the lives of the people mentioned in this book.

It is my desire that the glories of the past in Wales may bring new hope to all that love the Lord Jesus Christ. Every journey I take to Wales makes me pray for a true movement of God in the principality as I cross the border from England; it is my wish that every man, woman and child old enough to understand will learn the great value they have in their Christian heritage, which in my opinion is second to none. The Reverend Brian H. Edwards in his book *Revival!: A People Saturated with God*[3], writes, 'A book must be judged on its intention.' My intention is that the glories of the past will show the reader what God does when believers are brought into a deeper relationship with Him through the sanctifying work of the Holy Spirit. God is looking for a holy people. I pray that this book may bring an earnest prayer from the lips of the reader for true revival in the Church today that is built on a foundation of truthful biblical teaching and a love for our Saviour and Lord.

One last word: I have included three portraits and photographs of statues of my three heroes, Griffith Jones, Daniel Rowland and Thomas Charles; as photography had not then been invented, these representations may not be very accurate and do not make them look very happy! Their hairstyles and the clothes they wore were not like ours. As you read this book try and picture them in your mind as present-day people, because except for dress and hairstyle they were just like us.

After an initial introduction of our heroes I refer to them by their Christian names.

*Christopher J. Tokeley, Farnborough, Hampshire, UK, 2021*

**Notes:**

1. Recordings can be purchased from the Faith Mission, Edinburgh.

2. The Keswick Convention Week, 1955, Marshal, Morgan & Scott Ltd, London, 1955.

3. Brian H. Edwards, Evangelical Press, Darlington, 1990.

# CHAPTER 1

# GRIFFITH JONES, 'MORNING STAR' OF THE EVANGELICAL REVIVAL IN WALES

*'But God has chosen the foolish things of the world to shame the wise, and God has chosen the weak things of the world to shame the things which are mighty.'*

1 Corinthians 1:27

Born in a humble home to godly parents, Griffith Jones ministered so powerfully to the illiterate people of the principality of Wales that through his Welsh circulating schools they became known as the most literate in Europe. Their textbook was the Welsh Bible, from which they learned to read, and it brought them to faith in the Lord Jesus Christ and sowed the seed for the great revival that was to come. They had a burning desire for the Word of God in their own language.

The birth of a son to John ap Griffith (English: John son of Griffith) and Eleanor (Elinor) John, his wife, at Pant-yr-fel farm, in the parish of Penboyr, was their great joy. His baptism took place on 1 May 1684 at the neighbouring parish church of Cilrhedyn, shortly after the death of his father. Cilrhedyn is about ten miles south-east of Cardigan. Young Griffith must have been a great consolation to his mother in those days of her bereavement. He had no special education and attended, with other children, the village school when his poor health permitted.

As it was in the prophet Samuel's day, so it was in Griffith Jones' Wales: 'The word of the Lord was rare in those days; there was no widespread revelation' (1 Samuel 3:1). Like the young

Samuel, God spoke to Griffith. He kept sheep, like young King David, in the green picturesque rolling hills a few miles south-west of Newcastle Emlyn. During this period of his life, according to two of his biographers he had a vision or hallucination, possibly caused by his asthma. He first had a picture in his mind of the glory of heaven, and then the most terrible apparition of hell with multitudes moving towards eternal destruction. It seemed that practically the whole Welsh people were destined for eternal destruction and that he had been called upon by God to be an instrument to bring them to salvation. Others have said that he was kneeling in a field praying when he had a vision of the risen Christ, who told him of his mission in life. 'Behold, I will do something in Israel at which both ears of everyone who hears it will tingle' (1 Samuel 3:11). These words might well have been spoken to Griffith.

From that point on, his mind was set on God. Keeping sheep could not satisfy Griffith's spirit; uppermost in his mind and laid on his heart at a very early age was a God-given desire to be a shepherd of men. He later wrote, 'Oh! How many, yes, how many thousand souls are among us, who are ignorant, who, if asked about what they profess, can give no account whatever?'

Griffith's education was improved under John Maddocks at Carmarthen Grammar School, where his studies included Latin and Greek. His friends noted how often it was he set himself apart for a time of earnest prayer. When he was old enough he was encouraged by his pastor, Evan Evans, Vicar of Clydeu (Clydey), Pembrokeshire, to apply for ordination in the Church of England. To a young man whose eyes were already fixed on his Saviour this advice was a great encouragement. After being rejected as too young for the Anglican ministry he was employed to learn woodcarving. A further application was successful and he was ordained a deacon by Bishop George Bull on 19 September 1708 at the age of twenty-four.

Those close to Griffith were aware that God had His hand upon him. It is said by his biographer that 'He had a strong and intelligent mind; he had also a feeling heart, deeply imbued with a zeal for God, with the love of the Saviour, and with love for souls.' In 1708 his first curacy took him to Penbryn, a small coastal village nine miles north of Cardigan. This beautiful stretch of coast, now owned by the National Trust, was used as a location in the James Bond 007 film *Die Another Day*. Then Griffith moved on to Penrhiw parish, seven miles south-east of Cardigan, where the noble Philipps family had in the past owned a private chapel, now derelict. This young curate could not have known that this famous family would feature so much in his life. They could trace their ancestry back to the twelfth-century Wogan knights, whose tombs grace St David's Cathedral. The family liked to spell their name with one l and two p's to make it different from others of similar name. They would play a pivotal role in his life. The same year his curacy moved to Laugharne at the mouth of the River Taf. He was inducted as Rector of Llandeilo Abercywyn on 13 July 1711 and served there five years.

We know little about his life during this period of his early ministry, but we can be assured that like the Apostle Paul in Arabia (Galatians 1:17) he was being prepared by God for his future ministry while teaching and preaching the gospel. While there he came to the notice of the Bishop of St David's, Adam Ottley, who summoned him to appear at the Ecclesiastical Court on 8 May 1714 to account for his 'going about preaching on weekdays in Churches, Churchyards, and sometimes mountains, to hundreds of auditors'. The previous year Adam Ottley had been promoted from Archdeacon of Shropshire, England, and therefore thought he saw the need to show his authority and rein in this young overexuberant cleric, presumably before he turned Wales upside down. Ottley on his arrival the previous year to take up his new appointment was astounded at the dreadful state of his palace and decided to commission a dilapidation report. He was more interested in bricks and mortar than the spiritual state of his diocese!

The clergy were poor and some moved to parishes in England that provided better livings. Those curates left in the care of parishes in the principality often found additional work to augment their paltry stipends. This state of affairs resulted in a decline in standards among the clergy and apathy among their parishioners.

Although many attended church services, their span of attention was limited and drunkenness, revelry and fighting took place in the churchyards before and after services. There was also much superstition, and cockfighting sometimes took place on the north side of churches because it was considered by the superstitious to be a less sacred place than the side facing east. The spiritual life in many parishes had collapsed, but there were some praiseworthy exceptions.

The sermons of faithful pastors like Griffith yielded a small but precious harvest of souls. When God calls a man for a particular purpose He often chooses those who human-resources managers would reject. All his life Griffith suffered from ill health, and it is surprising that he was able to accomplish the mighty work to which he was called by God.

During his parish ministry he was seeking God's perfect will for his life. He was invited to consider missionary service in the Portuguese East Indies, with the East India Mission. On 18 June 1713 he stood before the committee of the SPCK in London as a candidate for the post of schoolmaster at the settlement of Tranquebar. He was to set sail for Tranquebar (Tharangambadi) on the east coast of India, known as the Coromandel Coast. Tranquebar means 'Land of the Singing Waves' and it is in the Indian state of Tamil Nadu. He purchased a Portuguese primer and also learned Spanish in order that he could know the basics of the local trading language.

This coast was dotted with Portuguese and Dutch forts, but by the eighteenth century it had fallen into the hands of the Danes. The town was occupied mainly by Indo-Portuguese merchants. His bags were packed, but he knew there were many in Wales ignorant of the Gospel. God was calling him and preparing him for a work that could only be done through the power and work of the Holy Spirit – it was to be in his homeland of Wales.

Under the guidance of the Holy Spirit he may have reflected on the state of his own country. God knew there was no one else quite as suited for His work in Wales. He could not turn his back on the dreadful state of his own people for those of a foreign country. Jesus said, "No one who puts his hand to the plough and looks back is fit for service in the Kingdom of God." We shall never know the wrestling within his own spirit that took place between him and God. Perhaps like Jonah he had accepted the invitation to Tranquebar to distance himself from the place where God wanted him to work. He knew unless he surrendered his life totally to God he would never have true peace in his heart. After months of soul-searching he wrote to the SPCK on 22 November 1713 declining their invitation. Unknown to him, his decision was to turn the spiritual tide in Wales from low to high. Griffith summed up the moral state of the principality with these words:

> The growing profaneness and open debauchery, the professed and practised infidelity, with the natural offspring of all this, the vices and immoralities of the time we live in, are so daring and barefaced as publicly to triumph in our streets, and bid defiance to the laws of God and man; the infectious fumes of pernicious errors and deadly works of darkness, which have too much eclipsed the gospel light already, and threaten the total extinction of it in our land; these dreadful calamities, I say, should awaken all the serious friends of religion to bestir themselves and exert their zeal for the preservation and revival of it before it quite forsake us, or is taken away in judgement from us.

Sir John Philipps in a letter to his friend Griffith Jones wrote:

> I believe there has scarcely been any age since the first publication of the Gospel when men talked or wrote so irrationally (that is of the subject of religion) and lived and held more immorally than at the present time.

Griffith Jones added to his reply, 'The enemy is coming in like a water flood.'

These quotations could describe our nation today. Griffith believed that 'The growth of vice and debauchery is greatly owing to the gross ignorance of the principles of the Christian religion.' These are his tough words and they showed his abhorrence of sin and the decadence of the society in which he lived, from which he previously may have wanted to escape.

# CHAPTER 2

## FAMILY AND FRIENDS UNITED IN CHRIST

*'Always in every prayer of mine making request for you all with joy, for your fellowship in the gospel from the first day until now.'*
Philippians 1:4–5

God knows those He can trust with the sacred task of supporting and funding the work of proclaiming the gospel. One was Sir John Philipps (4th Baronet) of Picton Castle, near Haverfordwest, Pembrokeshire, who was to become a close friend and patron of Griffith. He gifted him the benefice of Llanddowror, from where his literacy programme was administered. The stipend of £38 that Griffith received was considered as passing rich – the normal stipend was £25 or even less! Sir John was also supporting George Whitefield at Oxford at this time and was encouraging John and Charles Wesley and others in their spiritual growth.

The life of this Christian man is noteworthy. He was educated far from Wales at Westminster School and then at Cambridge University. He was a lawyer and admitted to Lincoln's Inn. Then in 1695 he was made Member of Parliament for Pembroke. Two years later he married Mary Smith[1], the heiress of a wealthy East India merchant, Anthony Smith. Mary was born in 1675 in Surat, India, the main trading port for the East India Company on the west coast, where her father was stationed. The marriage injected much needed capital that enabled Sir John to undertake repairs and renovations to their home, Picton Castle. In the year of his marriage to Mary he created a new front entrance to Picton Castle by a raised terrace at first-floor level, giving direct entry to the Great Hall, which was the main living room and dining room of the medieval castle. Before this alteration, access was via the vaulted undercroft twelve feet below the present level. The Great Hall, with its grand clocks, pictures, furniture and huge pedimented doorcases, and the chapel set above the entrance hall – this was the opulence that Griffith Jones would have viewed on being invited to his patron's home.

Sir John was generous in supporting good causes, which earned him the nickname the Good Sir John. He gave to the Society for the Reformation of Manners, the Society for Promoting Christian Knowledge (SPCK) and the East India Mission; in addition he sponsored two editions of the Bible in Welsh. He was a friend of John and Charles Wesley, and Sir Christopher Wren, with whom he worked as a church commissioner for building fifty new churches in London as the metropolis expanded eastwards. He was Member of Parliament for Haverfordwest from 1718 to 1722. He provided the finance for building the Old Bridge in Haverfordwest. The bridge, completed in 1736, replaced the ford which gave the town its name. He also provided the timber for the organ loft and gallery in St Mary's Church, Haverfordwest. On his death his sons erected a monument to Sir John; the year of his death is shown as 1736[2]. He was an influential in society and used his position to advance the cause of Christ.

Another benefactor whom Griffith first met together with her two sisters and her brother, Richard, when she was still a teenager was Bridget Vaughen, of Derllys Court, Llannewydd, Carmarthenshire. Her father, John Vaughen, was a patron of the SPCK and funded some of their schools among other charitable works. Griffith accepted invitations to preach at the services at their church at Merthyr. The beautiful and intelligent Bridget married Arthur Bevan, a lawyer and the Member of Parliament for Carmarthen on 30 December 1721. The marriage was a grand affair and the dowry and other gifts amounted to over £1,000. Bridget was converted under the ministry of the Reverend David Jones (Llanllwch), the nephew of Griffith Jones. She was keen to make known her evangelical faith to those in society as she entertained them. She was a charming person, which enabled her to make friends with those in society and to give wise advice to Christian men and women who were often her seniors. She inherited a considerable fortune in estates and was able to live in style at her residences in Carmarthen and Bath. With the income she carried on supporting charitable work, and from 1731 helped finance the Welsh circulating schools. Bridget Bevan was reported to have an annual income of £500 and much of it went into Christian work.

The friendship between Griffith and Bridget grew over the years and there was a regular exchange of correspondence. Although he was well educated it was quite natural that the former shepherd boy should seek her advice on how to conduct himself when moving among society and what topics he should bring into conversation.

It was not expected for a lady of her time to be well educated or capable of intelligent conversation. Ladies were expected to be engaged in idle gossip and petty intrigue with only the womenfolk. She was other than that – she could take on in debate the likes of the atheistic Lord Chesterfield. She had exceptional skills in handling her finances and administration of her estates. Even though she was rich her giving was sacrificial. She acknowledged that all her gold and silver came from God – as did King David, who proclaimed, 'Yours, O Lord, is the greatness and the power and the glory and the majesty and the splendour, for everything in heaven and earth is yours' (1 Chronicles 29:11).

Griffith and Bridget carried on an exchange of letters. Transcripts of Griffith's letters are preserved and show his gratefulness for her support, both financial and in prayer. His letter of 4 February 1738 shows how he was strengthened by her prayers.

> We met in Clydey a middling congregation. Several of whom I thought were a little affected with what they heard. The prayer of Persis [Madam Bevan] (Romans 16:12) which assisted me, will I hope yet prevail for a blessing.

Most of Griffith's letters are in the form of sermons to her and only briefly give personal details.

She very nobly and effectively carried on the administration of the schools after the death of Griffith until she died at the grand age of eighty-one years. Her faith shone through her life and she must be given her place of honour alongside her English contemporary the famous Countess Lady Huntingdon. There was a considerable correspondence between Griffith and Bridget about the schools and the well-being of Margaret, his wife, and she would send medicine to improve the health of both of them.

Another benefactor was Sir John Thorold, who was a friend of Lady Huntingdon. He wrote some of the prefaces in *Welsh Piety* and his name appears in the edition for 1745/46. *Welsh Piety* was the journal Griffith kept of the detailed account of his schools and was published annually. The name of Sir John Thorold is mentioned in the minutes of the SPCK from 1746 to 1749. Like John and Charles Wesley, he was a member of the Methodist Society that met in Fetter Lane in the City of London. His death occurred in 1748 and was a great loss to the Methodists. Griffith valued his wise counsel and the fellowship of these fine Christian friends.

These members of society were to make a very great contribution to the work of the Welsh circulating schools. Without their contribution from their wealth, their wisdom and friendship, it is unlikely that so much could have been accomplished in the principality and beyond. God has His rich and obedient servants in each generation to support and nurture His work. Because of their standing in society his preaching and work with the schools was kept from attack from those authorities, Church and civil, who saw them as a threat to the status quo. The SPCK provided books for the schools, and the benefactors caught the vision for the promotion of the gospel in Wales. The vision was not just to bring literacy to Wales. Griffith firmly believed that the vehicle of literacy would bring a change of heart of the people towards the Lord Jesus Christ. Through acceptance of the gospel would come reform of morals. The SPCK had objectives that were in accord with his vision. Griffith was in a position to obtain help from them because he was their trusted 'correspondent' and Sir John was an elected member of their committee.

Griffith accepted the benefice of Llanddowror, Carmarthenshire, from Sir John Philipps in the summer of 1716. Two years later Sir

John invited him to accompany him during July and August on a tour of Wales and Scotland. During this tour Griffith was to preach and the two men got to know one another as brothers in the proclamation of the gospel. Sir John also had ample opportunity to learn more of the merits and character of Griffith. During his curacy at Laugharne under the Reverend Thomas Philips[3], Sir John and Bridget Bevan had often heard good reports of Griffith Jones.

The bond of friendship between Griffith and the Philipps family was increased by two great events. The first was Griffith's marriage to Sir John's sister Margaret[4] in 1720. Since the death of his father, Erasmus Philipps, Sir John had inherited the baronetcy. He was in the position of sanctioning his sister's marriage to Griffith, the former shepherd boy of Pant-yr-fel, now Rector of Llanddowror. Margaret was nine years older than Griffith, who was thirty-seven years of age on their marriage. It seems she was a 'solitary and often sick woman'. Certainly most observers agree her health was not good, but she was described by others as a pious and charitable woman. Griffith saw her as a lifelong companion who shared her relatives' vision for the schools and their desire for a turn in the spiritual tide in Wales for good. Margaret did not live to see their prayers answered by the revival that began in Wales seven years later; she died on 5 January 1755. Her death was a tragic loss of companionship to Griffith when the schools were greatly increasing in number, with over 7,000 pupils in attendance that year. The second great event was the marriage of another sister, Arabella, to Richard Vaughen of Derwydd. Richard Vaughen was Bridget Bevan's uncle. All these Christian folk were related by marriage. God was certainly at work in bringing these influential families together!

During the early part of their marriage, Margaret had a live-in companion, Mary Francis. They shared the same interests in music and literature, so their time together must have been a great help to Margaret when Griffith was away from home and his time was taken up with his ministry in the Church and with the advancement of the Welsh circulating schools. The companions took a great interest in the progress of the growing Methodist movement and the quickening pace of the work of the Holy Spirit. They witnessed the changes in corporate worship that were slowly taking place with the introduction of new hymns and tunes. Mary was a good musician and was also gifted with a fine singing voice, so this must have been a great inspiration to Margaret.

Margaret's companion, Mary, was courted by the Reverend William Williams of Pant-y-celyn, who was the great hymn composer and writer of the Evangelical Awakening in Wales. The regular companionship between Mary and Margaret came to an end when William and Mary married in 1749; William was thirty-two years of age.

Griffith and Margaret held open house and many visitors came for advice and counselling. One visitor who called for advice was a young man, Howell Harris from Talgarth, who joined them for family worship at 9 a.m. on 8 March 1740. He was so impressed by the time he had with them that he wrote in his diary:

> O my leanness! O my leanness! How little do I yet know of the Glorious Majesty, and the hell within me. I want far more assurance that Christ was mine. O when shall I feel him fully and clearly filling every faculty of my soul in his nature, temper, spirit, holiness, wisdom, simplicity, strength, humility, love.

At this time in his life Howell Harris was an itinerant preacher. What did he learn from Griffith? He wanted to know Christ more intimately. During this time he was introduced to the talented Madam Bridget Bevan, and heard Griffith preach the gospel and was invited to do so himself. She gave him a pocket Testament.

The Philipps and Vaughen families were not only bonded in their marriages, but also in the God-given vision to bring the gospel message to their country. Private patronage offered to Griffith gave him advantages denied to the evangelical leaders that came after him in Wales. It was his love for his Lord and Saviour that secured him the patronage of the influential evangelical laity who shared his vision. God was laying the foundation that would release the dynamic power of the gospel throughout Wales.

**Notes:**

1. Marriage date 12.12.1697.

2. The year of the death of Sir John Philipps in many books is shown as 1737. That would appear to conflict with his memorial, which states the year 1736. When Sir John died Britain had not adopted the Gregorian calendar; we were still on the Julian calendar. The Gregorian calendar was introduced in 1752 and adjustments were made accordingly. This also applies to the date of the marriage of Griffith Jones to Margaret Philipps.

3. Some biographers of Griffith Jones have written that the Reverend Thomas Philips was the son of Sir John Philipps, 4th Baronet of Picton. Thomas Philips, whose surname is spelt three difference ways in church records, was the son of John of Carmarthen Town (CCEd Record 274846). Furthermore, the Reverend Thomas Philipps does not appear on the Philipps Family Tree.

4. Margaret Philipps was the daughter of Sir Erasmus Philipps (3rd Baronet) and Lady Catherine D'Arcy, Sir Erasmus's first wife, Lady Cecily Finch, died in 1658. They had three sons: Erasmus, John (Sir, 4th Baronet) and Bulkeley (*Dictionary of Welsh Biography*). Margaret is not mentioned on the Philipps family tree.

# CHAPTER 3

# GRIFFITH JONES, THE CARING PASTOR

*'He said to him again a second time, "Simon, son of Jonah, do you love Me?" He said to Him, "Yes, Lord; You know that I love You." He said to him, "Tend My sheep."'*

John 21:16

Griffith is most remembered in Wales for his work in education. It is not recorded when God put it into his mind to bring literacy to Wales. There can be no doubt that during the early years of his ministry he realised his congregation's understanding of the Bible was retarded by their illiteracy. He taught his congregation from the Bible in his sermons. Some said that his knowledge of the scriptures was extraordinary, as those under his ministry constantly heard him refer to biblical texts in his teaching. His mind was a storage of Bible verses that he could readily recall and use in his teaching and counselling. A biographer described his use of scriptures as being in a most 'appropriate manner' which his parishioners were glad of and could comprehend.

He gave much attention to the preparation of his sermons. They were well written, his delivery was engaging, his voice attractive, his manner serious and his delivery impressive. He preached from the heart in a manner that showed the utmost concern for his hearers. Whenever he spoke to his congregation he was earnest and tender, and some said he engaged them with a 'holy ardour'. He was a good conversationalist, persuasive and winsome, and no doubt God used these gifts to gain the confidence of his parishioners. Wherever he preached in churches or in the open air his preaching was with clear reasoning and sound arguments. It was serious, authoritative and powerful. A power which could only have come from the Holy Spirit turned his words into divine medicine and applied it to listening souls. His congregations increased and thousands began to gather in churches and in the open air to hear him.

He not only wanted his flock to know the Lord Jesus Christ as their personal Saviour and Lord, but he cared for their physical needs as well. Many ministers of religion were apothecaries. This required seven years of training and a final examination before recognition was given by the Society of Apothecaries. Griffith had the basic equipment for mixing the medicines that he ordered from London. When a typhus epidemic broke out in South Wales and many in his parish suffered and some died, Griffith was there for them. He felt deeply for their physical condition. He saw their need for adequate food incorporating a nutritious diet and for warm clothing as well as the more desperate spiritual need of those who faced death without the knowledge of salvation in Jesus Christ.

On the Saturday preceding the monthly Sunday Holy Communion service he would gather his congregation and prepare them. He would carefully explain the service and go through the Bible readings verse by verse. He would in a most kindly and loving manner draw out from his people the questions they had in their minds. In this way he found those who needed salvation or those who were partaking of the bread and wine in ignorance or for some unworthy reason. In addition he helped them to commit Bible verses to memory, and as an encouragement he gave them a dole of bread for their effort. His heart was moved when he knew his folk were unable to read the Bible for themselves. The cost of bread was paid out of the Holy Communion offerings that were due to him, as was finance to resource schools where both adults and children could be taught in their native tongue – Welsh.

# CHAPTER 4

# PERIPATETIC TEACHERS FOR WELSH CIRCULATING SCHOOLS

*'You therefore, my son, be strong in the grace that is in Christ Jesus. And the things that you have heard from me among many witnesses, commit these to faithful men who will be able to teach others also.'*

2 Timothy 2:1–2

Griffith's establishment of what were to become known as Welsh circulating schools was under way. The great majority of Welsh people were illiterate. There were few schools that were available to the poor, and the economic circumstances that prevailed made it impossible to allow time away from the daily task of earning or gathering enough food to keep body and soul together. According to Griffith 'Ignorance is the mother and nurse of impiety.' Therefore learning the truth through literacy was the way to knowledge and a godly life.

He had teaching experience in the SPCK school while curate at Laugharne and knew the difficulty that existed in teaching in English when the pupils' first language was also his – Welsh. He founded his first Welsh school in 1731 at Llanddowror while he was rector. By 1737 there were thirty-seven schools where about 2,400 pupils had attended. Even in the sparsely populated countryside, schools spread quickly. In the winter of 1738/39 schools were opened in Ynysybwl with forty-nine pupils and Pontypridd with forty pupils. By 1741 a school came to the folk at Cwm-mainllwyd, Cilybebyll, in Pontardawe, and began with twenty-six pupils.

Expansion continued apace with schools in 1748 at Llanelli. Then schools were held at nine farms in the Amman Valley, where an average of between thirty-four and seventy-four pupils attended. So the schools multiplied. Today many communities are proud to trace their beginnings of basic formal education to Griffith Jones and his Welsh circulating schools.

The establishment of circulating schools shows Griffith's business skills were quite remarkable in the days before the telephone, motorised transport, computers, and a reliable postal service. He must have been a genius at organisation. With the backing of several benefactors, he threw his energy into developing the schools in his forty-seventh year, when most ministers would not have taken on all the extra work in addition to their pastoral duties. Some have described him as a workaholic who suffered from insomnia, but the truth is more likely that he was a man of great physical and mental energy who, like Florence Nightingale, was able to get through a busy life while limiting deep sleep to a relatively short period of only about four hours. This helped his sermon preparation and the quick recall of scriptures from memory that he needed when preaching in the open air. He had no sophisticated computer system to aide his memory as many of us do today!

Teachers were needed, and they had to be interviewed, trained and paid. Teachers were only paid after they had given a full report on the progress of their school, including the numbers attending and the details of the pupils. These Griffith recorded in an annual report he called *Welsh Piety*. Teachers were often attacked by angry mobs that were ignorant as to the benefits of literacy. As in so many places today in the developing world, the work was often under threat. Schools to teach reading and writing skills were abhorrent to some people who had selfish motives in keeping education from poor people working on the land.

The textbooks used were the Welsh Bible and Prayer Book and sometimes pamphlets that Griffith himself wrote. He did not need books on mathematics and geography, or handwriting copybooks, as his aim was to teach his pupils to read so that they could understand the gospel and come to faith in Christ. He was accused of using his schools for promoting the cause of Dissenters and Methodists. In time the increasing number of literate people listened more intelligently to what was preached and demanded better sermons because they could read the Bible for themselves and discuss the sermons their ministers gave. All this resulted in a better understanding of the Christian faith. Statistics of the day showed that Holy Communion instead of being a rarity in some parishes increased to one celebration each month. Sometimes Griffith travelled by horse to remote parts of Wales to interview teachers and often to make arrangements for the schools. The venues of the schools depended on the generosity and disposition of the local clergy and gentry. He trained the masters of the schools by bringing them to his home in Llanddowror. There he established a small college and a place for the trainees to board. There was a small cottage called Yr hen Goleg (translated, The Old College), and a house called Plas y Bechgyn (The Boys' House).

He took a personal interest in every school as his letter to Madam Bevan dated 8 January 1737 shows; he was prepared to travel to visit the schools, and he also took the opportunity to preach the gospel. He had received a visit from Mr Thomas of Puncheston (Pembrokeshire) and agreed to visit his school.

> I have paved the way to go to examine his school without offence, which I am glad of, for I cannot be satisfied without knowing what is everywhere done with the charity I am trusted with. I have now a prospect of giving a sermon there at the same time.

### Rules of the Welsh Schools, As Laid Down by Griffith Jones, 18 February 1744/45

The masters must be sober, God-fearing, members of the Church of England, loyal to the King and the Government, and such as devote themselves sincerely to their work; not strolling about needlessly and idling about the place; not contending about controversial questions of Religion, nor following any customs opposed to the Word of God, the Law of the Land, or the order of the Church, nor interfering in anything unconnected with their calling; but keeping the following rules exactly & honestly.

31

1. That the masters, besides teaching their scholars to spell, and read such books as are appointed them, should teach them also, and question them carefully, twice every day, in the Church Catechism, and in its meaning as given in the printed commentary which is in use in the schools; and should give a few passages from it, every night, to the scholars to learn by heart for the next day; helping them to understand the meaning and significance of it as far as they can, and to train the scholars to make the responses to the minister carefully, reverently, and devotionally, in the Church service, from the Common Prayer at the Catechism, that they may as early and as often as possible come to say their Catechism to the minister of the parish.

2. That the masters & scholars should take care to come early to school every day, and continue diligently till evening, and come constantly to public worship every Sabbath. And the masters should question the scholars every Monday about the Chapters, the text, and the headings of the sermon which they heard in church the day before, and set themselves reverently and seriously to sing a psalm, and pray to God, together in school, every morning and evening. They should pray daily for the charitable subscribers to these schools, and for the blessing of God on those who are taught in them. The masters should warn their scholars earnestly against all bad habits, such as swearing and cursing, taking the name of God in vain, breaking the Sabbath, telling lies, and the like; and should exhort them to shun the company of wicked men, and the vain sinful pleasures of the world, and to turn to God, through faith in Christ, from all false and vain conduct. They should behave themselves charitably, reverently, humbly, and meekly towards all men; they should be industrious and faithful in their work, and in the errands and duties of their situations. In particular, the children should reverence, obey, and honour their parents; servants should be obedient, industrious, and faithful in the work and cause of their masters; and they should pray God every day, by themselves in private, for the grace of God to help them in everything, exerting themselves also as far as possible in meekness and wisdom, to exalt the worship of God in the families where they live.

3. The masters should keep and give in at the end of their quarter, or before the end of the following month at latest, a correct register of their scholars, their names, ages, the books they are reading, and the time (i.e. the number of months and weeks) each

scholar has spent in the school; how much of the Exposition of the Catechism they have learnt; as well as the name of the place, the parish & county, where the schools were; when the school began & ended, with the master's name. The master should obtain a certificate from the minister of the parish, or at any rate from the supervisors of the school, and such others as are truly honest, approved, and well-known in the neighbourhood. Provided that the schoolmasters follow these Rules exactly, and carry them out honestly, they are promised the customary wages, according to the number of scholars and the time they have been in school. And, therefore, the masters who come into this work should see that they are diligent & regular, that they may not fall into guilt and so be unable to answer before God, and, moreover, be paid no wages.

Together with the rules, the masters of the schools took with them letters of introduction signed by Griffith which were to be exhibited as an authorisation for them to teach in the parish with the prearranged permission of the incumbent.

Griffith was most concerned that his teachers should be persons devoted to the Lord Jesus Christ, and secondly they should be good teachers. In *Welsh Piety* for 1745/46 he stated:

All possible care is taken, that none be employed as Masters or Mistresses in the Schools, but such as are not only tolerably well qualified to teach to read, but such as appear to have more religious impression upon their minds than is common; and whoever of them discovers contrary disposition (as two only, I think, have done this year) they are to be discharged immediately. Many of the masters now are such as have themselves been taught in these schools.

We learn from this extract that teachers could be men or women, and that many were former pupils of the Welsh circulating schools.

There is no doubt that these men and women were inspired by Griffith and his method of instruction. They caught his vision for Wales, and they were prepared to teach literacy and follow the Lord Jesus Christ even though this meant hardship. He was able to persuade men like John Jenkin, who was a good bootmaker and poet, to leave his trade to teach in his schools. Schools met between September and May for four or five hours a night, or by day. Three times as many scholars came at night as in the day. A school would meet for three months. In *Welsh Piety* he wrote:

> In many of the schools adult people made about two-thirds of the scholars; of whom several were aged, who could not see without spectacles, two or three about sixty years. A few blind persons attended the catechetical instruction of the schools; one of whom made very remarkable improvement and is now assisting to catechise others.

All this activity must have put great demands on the teachers and the SPCK, who produced Bibles, prayer books and literature written by Griffith.

Who would embark on a career where payment for services came only after results were seen or where there was the possibility that harm or injury might come to them from the mob? The pay was about £4 a year. Masters would be called, sarcastically, 'enthusiasts' and later 'Methodists' by the ignorant mobs that would chase and beat them brutally. Evan Williams of Ystradgynlais, in reading Bunyan's 'Come and Welcome to Jesus Christ' (a discourse on John 6:39), was soundly converted – so much so that he began preaching the gospel with others round the villages. He put himself under the tutorship of Griffith Jones and was sent in 1742 as a tutor to North Wales. He was a strong well-built young man, but was so brutally beaten in Caernarvonshire that it destroyed his health, and as a result he died after a long illness on 20 August 1748 at only twenty-nine years of age. He suffered the enmity of the fiddlers and harpers, who lost their Sunday trade owing to his school. Evan Williams followed in the footsteps of the apostle Paul, who upset the silversmiths at Ephesus when they lost their trade (Acts 19:38). Griffith wrote:

> The kingdom of grace, which commences in this world, will end in the kingdom of glory in the next. Hence the reign of Christ is said to be forever.

This is a most suitable epitaph for those who engaged in this work.

Peripatetic schools were God's work. He provided all that was needed, and there was a surplus! The cup of His grace was full and running over.

What began in a small way in Carmarthenshire, in the benefice of Llanddowror, to teach literacy, encompassed Wales and laid the foundation for a spiritual revival. Leading English evangelicals came to visit Wales (a land whose language they could not understand) to observe the mighty work of God. From the middle of the eighteenth century, well through to the following century, the Church in Wales was gripped by waves of powerful God-sent revival. The Bible was read by thousands in their own language, and demand for this precious book always outstripped supply. Jesus Christ was exalted and honoured, and with the coming of the Industrial Revolution men sang His praise while at work in the coal and slate mines and on the mountains of Wales. It is said by historians that the revival in the eighteenth century called the Evangelical Wakening saved Britain from a bloody revolution like that experienced in France (1789–92). In the history of Wales there has never since been such a long and continuous progress of revival in the Church as there was in the eighteenth century, and this must have contributed to the stability of the nation through into the next century as well. The amazing work that God accomplished through this Glorious Chain of three Christian men and their wives and companions we shall see extended far beyond the borders of Wales and encircled the world.

Griffith Jones, who made a great impact on the evangelists who closely followed him in their field, preaching, prepared the ground for the revival that was to follow. In his diary for 9 March 1739, four years after the conversion of Daniel Rowland, George Whitefield wrote:

> I think Wales is excellently well prepared for the Gospel of Christ. They have many burning and shining lights among both the Dissenting and Church ministers, amongst whom Mr. Griffith Jones shines in particular. No less than fifty Charity schools have been erected by his means, without any settled visible fund, and fresh ones are setting up every day.

From this Whitefield learned the value of education in the North American colonies for furthering the gospel – including work among the slaves, whom he nurtured and treated with great respect and generosity.

# CHAPTER 5

# A LOSS FELT MOST DEEPLY

*'But it was you, a man my equal. My companion and my acquaintance. We took sweet counsel together, And walked to the house of God in the throng.'*

Psalm 55:13–14

The sudden death on 5 January 1737 of Sir John at his London home at Bartlett's Building, Holborn, from what was probably a massive stroke, had a profound impact that caused Griffith to cast his faith even more firmly in his Lord and Saviour. His death came when the circulating schools were still in their early years. The death of his brother-in-law and benefactor was a great loss that he felt most deeply:

> Sir John Philipps' departure from us, and leaving the work he was engaged in, whose zeal and management was so necessary towards the success of it [Welsh circulating schools] gives me so great a concern, if not insuperable grief.

However, the schools continued. Griffith wrote to a friend regarding the younger pupils of his Welsh circulating schools:

> I can assure you, Sir, I am credibly informed that these little adepts [well-versed children], on Sundays at home, teach their aged parents the way to heaven.

The first records of Welsh circulating schools were published in *Welsh Piety* in 1737, but some thirty schools had been established earlier by Griffith with his own income. These schools met usually for three months in the winter, when farming was at low season. During this time, because of the method of teaching and the peculiarity of the Welsh language, those attending would have learned enough to enable them to read. The process of learning was continued after the school moved on by the more proficient teaching the less able. Enthusiastic children often returned home to teach parents or grandparents who were unable to attend the school because of household duties. This increased their knowledge of the scriptures and made a profound impact on their lives. The teacher of the school was only expected to teach from the Bible, prayer books and pamphlets written by Griffith Jones. The pupils were taught to sing psalms. They were expected to commit to memory what they were taught. Heavy demands were made on the resources of the SPCK for Bibles and prayer books in Welsh. *Welsh Piety* records that between 1737 and 1761 (the year of Griffith Jones' death) 3,495 schools had taken place in 1,200 different venues and 158,237 pupils had been taught (probably a good percentage of the population of Wales). The work continued, and records show that up to 1777 (the year of Madam Bevan's death) the number of schools recorded had increased to 6,465 and pupils to 314,051 in over 1,600 different places throughout Wales.[1] These are amazing figures when the population was somewhere between 390,000 and 450,000.[2] Some historians believe the number of those taught may be even higher! What a difference it would make in Wales or any country today if seventy-five per cent of the population were taught the Bible and committed much of it to memory!

It is not surprising that Wales was known as the most literate country in Europe! Even Catherine the Great, the Empress of Russia, made enquiries about the schools.

The circulating schools needed Bibles, prayer books and pamphlets. In July 1712, early on in the work of the schools and before records were published (perhaps they were not kept), Griffith received from the SPCK three dozen Welsh Bibles. However, the traffic was not one-way. In 1733 in response to an appeal from the SPCK, the Parish of Llanddowror contributed over £77 towards support of Protestants who had been evicted from Salzburg, Austria, by edict of Archbishop Firman.

The impact of the schools was very great; it was the springboard for the gospel. For many decades the Church in Wales experienced powerful movements of regeneration that can only be attributed to the work of the Holy Spirit working upon the foundations laid by Griffith, his teachers and his benefactors.

The growth of the circulating schools since records were kept in 1737 through to Griffith's death in 1761 were entered in *Welsh Piety*. Each year thousands of people, young and old, attended the schools. These may have been in various towns, villages, hamlets and farms during winter months, with different teachers in the evenings or daytimes.

In *Welsh Piety* for 1747/48 Griffith expressed his understanding that there were 20,000 people who would like to read the Bible. This demand could only be attributed to growth in literacy due the progress of the schools.

To give a snapshot of how much was organised and accomplished for just a few months each year, the following are details of the schools for the year 1738–39.

## Information provided from *Welsh Piety*, Written by the Reverend Griffith Jones

| County | Schools | Pupils |
|---|---|---|
| Brecknockshire | 6 | 332 |
| Cardiganshire[3] | 10 | 811 |
| Carmarthenshire | 9 | 584 |
| Glamorgan | 22 | 1266 |
| Merioneth (Bala) | 1 | 55 |
| Montgomeryshire | 5 | 274 |
| Monmouthshire | 4 | 186 |
| Pembrokeshire | 10 | 309 |
| Radnorshire | 4 | 172 |
| Total | 71 | 3989 |

**Notes:**

1. Figures from Geraint H. Jenkins, *The Foundations of Modern Wales, 1642–1780*, Clarendon Press, 1987, and F. A. Cavenagh, *The Life and Work of Griffith Jones*, University of Wales, Press Board, 1930.

2. The estimated population of Wales in 1700 was 390,000, and in 1750 it was 450,000 according to Peter D. G. Thomas in his *The Remaking of Wales in the Eighteenth Century*.

3. The Llangeitho and Llanddewi-Brefi parishes were under the care of the Rowland family.

# CHAPTER 6

# AN ITINERANT PREACHER AND FISHER OF MEN

*'And Jesus said to Simon, "Do not be afraid. From now on you will catch men."'*

Luke 5:10

Griffith Jones wrote, 'To be strong in faith, will make us strong in God's service – strong to do what he requires, to believe what he promises, and to persevere in prayer.' This could be said to be his mission statement and shows his strength of character.

To see the full picture of what God wrought through Griffith we need to look at the great accomplishment of his preaching. Although he was a rector of a parish, an author and supervised the circulating schools, he was also an itinerant preacher of the gospel. His zeal for the gospel took him by invitation into parishes other than his own, much to the annoyance of some clergy. He was preaching to as many as 4,000 people in the open air. He used the opportunities to preach at the Vanity Fairs held at Easter and Whitsun, for they provided a ready-made audience. There he often had a good response to the gospel message. He took every opportunity he had to preach the gospel wherever he could find a crowd.

If the congregations were too big for the church, he would preach in the open air. He was the first of the field preachers of the eighteenth century and gave wise advice to those who chose to do likewise. He carefully selected the place and the time he would preach. As his fame grew, the news that he was to preach soon reached the ears of the public and large crowds assembled to hear. He was a preacher and fisher of men in the tradition of the Apostles. A contemporary described his preaching in these words:

> Every word was like a fresh attack, carried with it a sort of triumphant accent . . . no wonder that his hearers wept, when the preacher himself burst into tears . . . no wonder that he was so successful in the conversion of sinners, when it was the divine Spirit that made the Word effectual.

Although he was called before the Bishop's court to account for his behaviour, God must have protected him and given him words of wisdom to speak as his licence was not withdrawn, unlike others that followed his example. He escaped with a proverbial slap on the wrist! But like the Apostles Peter and John when summoned before the Sanhedrin for healing the crippled man at the gate beautiful, he could not help speaking about what he had seen and heard (Acts 4:20).

Griffith was regarded as the greatest preacher in Wales, but he would be eclipsed by the conversion of a young cleric at Llanddewi-Brefi. One preaching engagement that certainly made a major impact on Wales took place in the large ancient collegiate church of Llanddewi-Brefi in the winter of 1734/35. This sermon was the great moment and turning point for God's blessing on the Church in Wales. Griffith could never have imagined how his sermon would be answered and what God would accomplish. God gave exceedingly above all that was asked! This young cleric who heard Griffith is my second hero in the Glorious Chain of events.

Griffith was not only a powerful preacher, a good organiser and loving pastor, but he was also a fine judge of character; he had a God-given instinct as to whether a man was living close to the Saviour and was a suitable candidate for teaching or serving those in the Church. This was shown in his choice of teachers for his schools – rarely after training were they rejected for the post. During May 1736 a young man from Talgarth, Howell Harris, who had recently been converted, visited Griffith at Llanddowror to seek his advice on ordination. As Griffith thought he was too young for ordination (born 23 January 1714) he advised him to find a teaching post, and in this he would give help. Howell had been awakened spiritually by the godly Vicar of Talgarth, Pryce Davies, on Palm Sunday 1735. He was made to think earnestly by the words addressed to the congregation concerning coming to the Communion table: "If you are not fit to come to the Lord's table, you are not fit to come to Church, you are not fit to live, you are not fit to die." This has been described as the arrow that pierced Howell Harris's conscience.

Although Howell Harris was never ordained because he was considered to be a Methodist, he became an itinerant preacher; he was always aware of the importance of education among his adherents. He founded the community at Trevecka and established societies for fellowship, prayer and Bible study throughout Wales. Nearby, Selina, Countess of Huntingdon, leased Isaf farmhouse from Howell Harris's brother Thomas and there founded a college for preachers. It was opened by her personally on 29 July 1768; she stayed with her entourage of ladies and servants over two months, and in the following years she visited on her birthday when most of the great Calvinistic Methodist leaders were there to preach.

It would be faithful to the times to explain that sometimes there were divisions between Griffith and others over doctrine, but these never dulled the Christlike love that his contemporaries, such as Howell Harris and Daniel Rowland, had for him and he for them. In a letter Howell Harris wrote to Daniel Rowland, he said:

> Last Sunday was a day of uncommon sweetness, light, love, liberty, and power, under the ministry of dear Mr. Griffith Jones, when many hundreds of the lambs gathered to meet the great Shepherd, and I believe they met him.

One person he chose to work alongside him was Howel Davies. Howel was converted through the ministry of Howell Harris. Howel Davies was sent to Talgarth to teach in a small school to rival one Howell Harris had already established in the village. Howell Harris was on fire for his Saviour. The two men met and the result was that Howel Davies found new life and forgiveness in Christ Jesus. The change in Howel's life was so dramatic that he applied for ordination (which his new friend had been refused). He was ordained deacon in 1739 and priest in the following year, serving under Griffith Jones at Llandeilo Abercywyn. On his ordination Griffith invited his congregation to unite in a special time of prayer for this young man, which they did with great enthusiasm. Howel Davies moved on to Pembrokeshire, where he made a great impact on the population that earned him the title the Apostle of Pembrokeshire; everywhere he went crowds gathered to hear him and many received the Saviour Jesus Christ gladly. He was one of the 'founding fathers' of Welsh Methodism, along with Howell Harris, Daniel Rowland, William Williams of Pant-y-celyn and Peter Williams.

A ministry as powerful as Griffith's could not go without notice by those opposed to the Kingdom of God. He had various absurd charges laid against him. The list was impressive, such as his parents were Nonconformists, he had studied Hebrew under a Presbyterian, he had distributed 24,000 copies of Matthew Henry's *Commentary*, and he had gone to great expense at putting down wakes, fairs and sports; none of these charges of course was true, but of few of them would one be ashamed. It has already been said that he was taken before a consistory court on the false charge of neglecting his parish. From this he was exonerated. The Reverend John Evans was the rector of the neighbouring parish of Eglwys Cymmin for fifty-one years, but was rarely there to perform his ministry! He was for forty years Reading Chaplain at Her Majesty's chapel at Whitehall, London. He wrote a pamphlet attacking Griffith Jones in 1749 and the following year in a sermon given to the Most Honourable and Loyal Society of Ancient Briton's[1] at St Andrew's, Holborn, made veiled attacks on the Rector of Llanddowror, accusing him of trying to destroy the Church. In his sermon he pleads for funds to establish his own school for Welsh children in London! This was an attempt on Evans' part to divert support given to the Welsh circulating schools to schools in London.

False rumours about Griffith were spread far and wide and

even those in high places became alarmed. He was cited by Queen Anne to preach before her as she had heard unfavourable reports on the substance and style of his preaching. Having heard him preach, he was bade farewell with the assurance that Her Majesty most heartily wished that every clergyman preached in the same manner. Ministers of the gospel who should have known better accused him of 'deluding ignorant men and leading captive silly women and children by despising the clergy'.

Here are some remarkable dates for those interested in the eighteenth-century Evangelical Awakening: Howell Harris was converted on 20 April 1735 (Whit Sunday), Daniel Rowland sometime in the autumn/spring of 1734/35, and George Whitefield during Lent 1735. What a glorious triumph of God's grace were those twelve months! The Wesley brothers were converted in May 1738 in Fetter Lane, City of London, the same year as William Williams of Pant-y-Celyn, known as the Sweet Singer of Wales, came under the preaching of Howell Harris. The impact of the Holy Spirit on those lives was so great that they could say with the apostle Paul, "Woe if I preach not the gospel" (1 Corinthians 9:16). These men changed the direction of the Welsh and English-speaking peoples towards God.

Bishop William Morgan, the principal translator of the Welsh Bible, gave the people of the principality the Bible in their own tongue; Griffith Jones, by teaching them to read Welsh, helped them to understand its teaching. Like Ezekiel's vision of a valley of dry bones (Ezekiel 37) that came to life, so the reading of God's word brought new life to the Church in Wales.

Since the death of Margaret, his wife, Griffith was lovingly cared for by Madam Bevan in her own home. He died after a short illness on 8 April 1761 and in his will he left £7,500 to the schools. William Williams, the poet and hymn writer, who knew Griffith Jones well because his wife had been a member of the household at Llanddowror, wrote his elegy. A few verses are quoted here, translated from the Welsh by the Reverend E. Morgan, Vicar of Syston, Leicestershire; the verses show in a microcosm the impact of his life and death.

# 1.

Cambria! hark, in sackcloth shroud thee,
   Linger not to shed thy tears,
Greater loss hast thou sustained
   Than forebode thy present fears.
One distinguish'd star from heaven
   Fell, and thou hast lost its ray;
Other stars in darkness wonder
   How its loss has dimm'd their day.

# 2.

When portentous clouds had darken'd
   Britain's Isle, and all was night,
'Twas the star that kindly bless'd us
   With a steady, heavenly light:
Zion's watchmen, on their pillows,
   Slept a fatal midnight sleep;
But the shout his trumpet sounded
   Made them holy vigils keep.

# 3.

Forth the gifted champion sallied,
   Preaching gospel truth around;
And in Jesu's name proclaiming
   Free Salvation's joyous sound:
Crowded thousands throng'd around him,
   Filling every sacred aisle;
And at length the churchyard seeking –
   Too confined the holy pile!

## 4.

Far to Scotland's northern mountains:
　　Urging on his glorious race,
Went his zeal aloud proclaiming
　　Leading-points of gospel grace:
Millions heard the heavenly herald
　　Preaching peace to fallen man;
And his lofty strains were welcom'd
　　By our Sovereign Lady Anne.

## 5.

Thirty thousand Bibles furnished,
　　Cambria, for thy thirsty land,
All prepar'd and well corrected,
　　By our zealous pastor's hand:
Two editions, by his bounty,
　　Shed their light to bless the poor;
And the sacred volume enter'd
　　At the humble cottage door.

## 6.

Providence, whose operations
　　Varied, beauteously entwine,
Knew a book for him was useless
　　That could never read a line:
'Stablished schools, from *Severn*'s fountain
　　To the *Western* Irish Sea;
Now the shepherd boy sits herding
　　With the Bible on his knee.

Schools three thousand bless'd thee, Cambria,
    Six score thousand pupils taught,
Toll to-day the noble triumph
    Which his earnest prayer sought:
Prom *Kheidiol*'s stream to *Severn*'s course
    Gospel light was kindled wide;
And from Cambria's lofty mountains,
    'Twas reflected on the *Clyde*.

**8.**

If thy shore around thee, Cambria,
    Measure full six hundred miles,
Where, in thick Egyptain darkness,
    Satan practised deadly wiles:
If a thousand parish bound'ries
    Mark thy circled surface o'er,
There, in native tongue, was taught thee
    How to read the sacred lore.

**9.**

In the North, where light was scantiest,
    Hostile pow'rs were long display'd,
To obstruct each kind endeavour,
    Which his ardent spirit made:
Yet where bigot zeal had triumph'd,
    Prudence all its force o'ercame;
Furious bears, and subtle foxes,
    Drank the Spirit of the Lamb.

The final words spoken by Griffith Jones show how he had suffered much from illness, but lived a fulfilled and fruitful life in living for his Lord, seldom complaining about his indisposition:

I must bear witness to the goodness of God. Oh, wonderful is the love of God to me, that I am now, even now, free from that troublesome distemper, the asthma, which I was subject to in my younger days, that I could not walk the length of this room but with the greatest difficulty. How wonderful is the love of God to me, that I am not blind, as I was for three weeks in my childhood, when I had the smallpox, and that I am not a blind beggar going from door to door! How wonderful is the love of God, that I have such a good friend [Madam Bridget Bevan] to take care of me, when I cannot help myself. How wonderful is the love of God, that I now feel so little pain, but that I am likely to go to my grave with ease. How wonderful is the mercy of God, that I can clearly see what Christ has done and suffered for me, and that I have not the least doubt of my interest [security] in my all-sufficient Saviour.

Madam Bevan continued the supervision of the schools' work until she died. Although she left a legacy of £10,000 for the schools in her will this was contested by two of the trustees, Lady Stepney and Admiral William Lloyd of Danytallt, Llangodock. One has to wonder what Lady Stepney's motives were, other than greed, as twelve years earlier she had inherited the Derwydd estate. They claimed the legacy as next of kin and so the fund was invested in the Court of Chancery. The action of the lady and admiral brought a sudden decline to the schools movement as there was not the money to pay teachers and nobody stepped in to repair the damage. It was a great loss to at least 10,000 pupils and did extreme damage to the power and prestige of the Church in Wales. With the loss of the schools in 1777 to the recovery of the legacy from the court in 1810 was one of the saddest periods for education in the history of the Church in Wales.

Charles Dickens wrote about the failures of the Court of Chancery and money-grabbing lawyers in his novel *Bleak House*. The lawyer's costs in Bleak House exceeded the legacy, and those who hoped for an inheritance were left penniless, but the hero, John Jarndyce, came to the rescue by providing for them. Perhaps it was the possible costs incurred that kept anyone from coming to the aid of the schools. Madam Bevan's legacy was to remain with the court for thirty years. The funds were unlocked during the lifetime of our third link in the chain, who came on the scene by an unexpected turn of events. God was to move again in a mysterious way indeed!

Bridget Bevan's final request was that her body should be buried beside that of Griffith Jones and Margaret, his wife, at Llanddowror – not at Merthyr, where she had married and worshipped God.

Griffith and Margaret, his wife, and their friends had sowed the seed that would grow and in time prepare the believers for the outpouring of the Holy Spirit in a mighty revival.

**Note:**

1. The Honourable and Loyal Society of Ancient Britons was a London-based Welsh cultural and philanthropic society, founded in 1715.

# CHAPTER 7

## DANIEL ROWLAND, A YOUNG CURATE BROUGHT UP WITH A START!

*'And if Christ is in you, the body is dead because of sin, but the Spirit is life because of righteousness.'*

Romans 8:10

Llangeitho, a small village in the beautiful Aeron Valley, was under the care of three generations of the Rowland family. Daniel senior was rector from June 1697 until his death in March 1731. He was a godly man who knew Griffith Jones and allowed Welsh circulating schools to be established in his parishes. He also during the latter years of his ministry preached the gospel in parishes other than his own by invitation of the incumbents. But it must have been a great burden held on his heart that his son named after him had not taken serious heed to the gospel. His eldest son, John, was ordained as deacon, serving as curate under his father at Llangeitho.

Daniel junior was born in the year 1713 at Pant-y-Beudy, in the Parish of Nantcwnlle (Llancwnlle), near Llangeitho, to the Reverend Daniel and Jennet Rowland. When he was a child he was miraculously saved from death when a large stone fell from the top of a chimney on to the spot where he had been sitting only minutes before. His early schooling was put in the care of Mr Pugh, who was well known for his scholarship. The school was at Pontigido near Llanarth, about twelve miles west of Llangeitho. The subjects Mr Pugh taught his pupils included Latin and Greek. Tradition has it that he was later educated at

Hereford Grammar School. He was eighteen when his father died; and the family were poor, so he did not go on to study at university as did his contemporaries. He was instituted as curate under the charge of his brother John, who became rector at Llangeitho and Nantcwnlle on his father's death. The ordination of Daniel took place at Duke Street Chapel, London, on 10 March 1733. Daniel walked all the way there from Llangeitho and back, which shows his determination and physical fitness, and also the fact that the family could not afford a horse or the expense of sustaining both on the journey. It is about 230 miles to London, and then there is the walk back! He possibly took the route used by drovers to sell their sheep at markets in London.

Like so many of the clergy of his time, Daniel was unaware of the need for the new birth. He was popular with his people due to his love for games and drinking, often leading to excess. Nearby at Llwynypiod was the independent congregation of Dissenters (a congregation of the Cilgwyn group of churches), whose minister was the Reverend Philip Pugh, who was preaching, among other subjects, about sin, law, wrath and judgement. Rowland had heard that some of his parishioners were attracted to the preaching of Mr Pugh, and therefore he decided to preach on similar subjects and searched the Bible for terrifying texts, such as 'The wicked shall be turned into hell', 'These shall go away into everlasting punishment' and 'The great day of His wrath is come.' His zeal and fervour was such that people soon began to pack the church. Crowds came to hear his preaching because of his notoriety, and some were awakened by his ministry although he himself was unregenerate. What Rowland did not realise was that Pugh also preached concerning the love, mercy and the grace of God shown in Christ Jesus.

In the winter of 1734/35 Daniel was one of many who gathered in the large church of Llanddewi-Brefi to hear the itinerant preacher Griffith Jones, Rector of Llanddowror, Carmarthenshire. At this time the parish of Llanddewi-Brefi, five miles east of Llangeitho, was in the care of Daniel's brother

John. It is uncertain why Jones was invited to preach in the parish, but it must have been by permission of John Rowland. Griffith seldom preached in parishes unless invited as he was intent on living within the rules of the Established Church. Some biographers have indicated that the congregation may have been assembled in the graveyard. There appears to be some confusion among the early biographers over the exact location but there can be no doubt that Jones' visit was to proclaim the gospel of our Lord Jesus Christ in no uncertain way. Little did he realise what the result of his preaching on that day would be!

The sermon was the instrument of Daniel's spiritual awakening. Griffith Jones saw the restlessness and arrogance in Daniel and, according to John Owen (his biographer), he was publicly challenged as to his spiritual condition directly by Jones. The preacher took the opportunity to break from his sermon and pray for the young curate. There and then he offered up a prayer to God that this young man would become an instrument of His glory.

At the time of Daniel's conversion, another young man, Howell Harris, was preaching in the open air and William Williams of Pant-y-celyn was one of his converts. With Howel Davies, they too were to become great friends of Daniel and co-workers for the Lord. They and others were God's instruments in the revival. The seed had been sown with the benefits of education through the establishment of societies, and support for Welsh circulating schools that had been pioneered by Griffith Jones.

Daniel was gripped by the gospel preached by Griffith Jones of Llanddowror, and after much soul-searching he surrendered his life to the claims of the risen Christ. His preaching became powerful and dynamic, but there was a need to preach about the grace as well as the justice of God. He was preaching on divine matters that worried him personally, and for some time he wrestled with these convictions that worried him. Soon, however, the preaching of this young curate was brought to the attention of Philip Pugh, who gave him good advice: 'Preach the Gospel to the people, dear sir, and apply the Balm of

Gilead, the Blood of Christ to their spiritual wounds and show the necessity of faith in the crucified Saviour.'

'I am afraid', said Rowland, 'that I have not that faith myself in its vigour and full exercise.'

'Preach on it,' said Pugh, 'till you feel it, in that way no doubt it will come. If you go on preaching the Law in this manner you will kill half the people in the country, for you thunder out the curses of the Law and preach in such a terrific manner that no one can stand before you.'

This advice struck home to his heart and brought him peace and full assurance of faith. Soon this kindly advice was taken up and made his ministry an even greater help to his parishioners.

He was ordained priest on 31 August 1735 at Abermarlais Chapel, on the estate of the wealthy Rice family at Llandeilo, and was appointed curate of Ystradffin, Carmarthenshire. He was deprived of this curacy in 1742, but gained the living of Llanddewi-Brefi. His last sermon at Ystradffin was on Acts 20 verse 32, 'And now, brethren, I commend you to God, and to the word of His grace, which is able to build you up, and to give you an inheritance among all them which are sanctified.' He wrote to Mrs James at Abergavenny, who was soon to marry George Whitefield, about his departure:

> I am suffered to be no longer at Ystrad-ffin! I preached my farewell sermon from Acts 20:32. It reached their hearts. I believe such crying out was not heard in say [at a] funeral in the memory of man. May the Lord hear their cry, and send them an able and powerful minister who will dispense to them the word of truth as it is in Jesus. I am now to settle at Llanddewi-brefi, which is a large church; it will contain several thousands of people [there was no seating for ordinary folk]. Several of my communicants at Ystrad-ffin will join there, and at Abbergwessin, the end of the month.

Daniel could not have realised at the time how the enforced move to Llanddewi-Brefi, not far from Llangeitho, would bring his ministry into greater focus. The two parishes were under the cure of his brother. For the next fifty years Daniel Rowland was to preach from the neighbouring parish of Llangeitho to thousands who flocked to hear him. His regular congregation numbered about 2,000, but on sacrament Sundays thousands more travelled to Llangeitho from as far as the Lleyn Peninsula. Some walked seventy miles and many came on horseback so that several fields were set aside as a paddock and horses were tethered to the hedgerows. Local people took in guests and many slept in barns for the night.

*Portrait of Griffith Jones.*

*Portrait of Madam Bevan.*

*Parish Church, Llanddowror, Carmarthenshire, Wales.*

*Picton Castle, Havefordwest, showing the 1790s extension.*

*Picton Castle showing 1697 raised terrace entry.*

*Picton Castle, the Great Hall – a magnificent room.*

# CHAPTER 8

# DANIEL ROWLAND, A PROPHET SENT BY GOD

'Behold, I say to you, lift up your eyes and look at the fields, for they are already white for harvest! And he who reaps receives wages, and gathers fruit for eternal life, that both he who sows and he who reaps may rejoice together.'

John 4: 35–36

'How thankful ought we to be that a harvest has been afforded us! A day of grace has been graciously vouchsafed to us,' wrote Griffith Jones of Llanddowror, who knew the time of sowing the seed of the gospel was giving way to the reaping of a mighty harvest of souls.

For over fifty years God drew thousands from all over Wales to witness the times of spiritual refreshing under the Reverend Daniel Rowland's ministry at Llangeitho. From 1735 Llangeitho became the centre from which revival ebbed and flowed. Some called Rowland the greatest preacher in Europe, and others, referring to him, wrote, 'in the pulpit, another Apostle Paul'. The evangelist Howell Harris wrote glowingly, suggesting that his gifts and calling to be a minister of Christ were 'beyond those of others'. Thousands would attend the services, and as a young man our third link in the Glorious Chain was converted under his powerful preaching. Over 100 Welsh clergy testified that their conversion to the Lord Jesus Christ was brought about through the preaching of Rowland.

Before we look at the life of young Daniel – or Dan, as he preferred to be called by friends, and as he signed his name – we must look at the history of the Church in Wales at this time. It had its great periods of triumph over evil, but it was a persecuted movement. Some of its leaders were to be deprived of their livings for preaching the gospel. They were also taken before magistrates on trumped-up charges and one was murdered, another blinded and many injured by the violence of mobs of ignorant men carrying clubs and guns, egged on by rich landowners who saw the Methodists as a threat to their selfish lifestyle. Seldom were the perpetrators brought to justice. Daniel, writing to his friend and companion in the gospel Howell Harris in October 1742, conveyed some disturbing news:

> I have been in Montgomeryshire, and I had great power there to convince and to build. *Persecution increases*, some of the brethren were excommunicated. I hope you will consult the brethren in London, and send us word what is best to do. Afterwards I preached with uncommon power in churches and several houses at Brecknock. I heard since that I have been put into the Ecclesiastical Court by Mr. Phillips of Builth, for discoursing at an ale-house there. Brother W[illiam]. Williams [Pant-y-celyn] is put in too, for not living in the parish where he officiates.

When preaching at Aberystwyth a man swore, shouting that he would shoot Daniel Rowland, but pulling the trigger it failed to fire. At another gathering an explosive charge hidden under hay was discovered in time, averting certain death to him and at least some of his congregation. It appears improvised explosive devices are not new!

It was not a time of ease for these young men who had come through divine revelation to know by faith the risen Lord Jesus Christ. Preaching of the Cross and the risen Christ often brought opposition and anger from the spiritually blind. Remember the early years of Saul of Tarsus! Jesus warned his disciples of persecution to come.

> They will put you out from the synagogue [the recognised place of worship]; yes, the time is coming that whosoever kills you will think he offers God service. And these things they will do to you because they have not known the Father nor Me. [John 16: 2–3].

# CHAPTER 9

## DANIEL PREPARES THE GROUND

*'He said to him again a second time, "Simon, son of Jonah, do you love Me?" He said to Him, "Yes, Lord; You know that I love You." He said to him, "Tend my sheep."'*

John 21:16

Following in the footsteps of Griffith Jones, early in his evangelical ministry Daniel gathered together as many of his congregation from Nantcwmlle that would come to a farmhouse called Gelly-Dywyll, owned by a tailor in the pretty valley of Bwlchdiwargan between that parish and Llangeitho. His aim was to teach them the true meaning of the Lord's Supper and to ensure they would eat and drink this sacrament worthily. He likewise called together those from Llangeitho. Sometimes these meetings were held in barns. This was a new experience for his people, but soon this teaching ministry was greatly appreciated and many gave testimony to the blessing they received. These meetings met weekly and were the equivalent of home groups today. Daniel had a quick and clear perception of the spiritual needs of his people. Daniel encouraged his people to search their own hearts as to their motives for taking the sacrament. He explained to them from the Bible that they needed to be prepared for the attacks of the Evil One, and they should also be aware of the needs of other Christians and take the gospel news to their neighbours.

These meetings became known as Societies. Daniel with his friends William Williams of Pant-y-celyn and Howell Harris, who was gifted with administrative skills, developed these Societies throughout Wales. The leaders of the Societies were gathered together in Associations four times each year in four different venues in North and South Wales. They were very much like our Church Conferences today. Ministers and lay preachers called exhorters were invited to attend. The Associations met for two days, which enabled the leaders to confer and review the work of the Societies. On day one, two sermons were preached at 4 p.m. and two at 6 p.m., interspersed with hymn singing. On the second day two sermons were preached at six in the morning and two later at 10 a.m. When it was heard the Associations were meeting, thousands would flock to hear the sermons.

Daniel would travel by horse to many places to preach, and he described his journey:

> We used to travel over hills and mountains on our little nags, without anything to eat but the bread and cheese in our pockets and without anything to drink but water from the springs.

He would serve his own congregation on Sundays, but during the week he was available to other churches. He served the parishes of Twregwyn, Wainifor, Abergorlech and Llanllian and his former curacy at Ystradffin for seven years.

# CHAPTER 10

# OPEN! WHAT MUST BE OPENED?

*"What hinders me from being baptised?" Then Philip said, "If you believe with all your heart, you may." And he answered and said, "I believe that Jesus Christ is the Son of God."*

Acts 8:36–37

It is recorded that a family member said that Daniel Rowland knew the Bible by heart and could give chapter and verse for any scripture quoted to him. His surviving daughter described him as being short in stature and having an iron constitution. His knowledge of the scriptures is shown in his sermons. In his sermon on Revelation 3:20, he quoted over forty-five other Bible passages in his passionate call to his hearers on behalf of his Lord to:

Open! What must be opened? The heart. Not only the door of our lips, but the door of our hearts must be opened. Indeed both must be opened – for our Saviour says, 'When you pray say;' [Luke 10:2] not only meditate, but speak with your tongues, yet the confession of the mouth and the belief of the heart must go together [Romans 10:10].

Before the close of his ministry many thousands were to thank God for his powerful preaching, including a young man by the name of Thomas Charles, whose ministry was blessed by God with a mighty work of the Holy Spirit. This young man from Carmarthenshire is our third link in this Glorious Chain. Towards the end of the eighteenth century the number of Welsh clergy who had been blessed by Daniel and his friends had risen to about eighty per cent of the total. Only occasionally did Daniel venture outside Wales. He knew that the evangelisation of England was in the domain of his friend George Whitefield, and when he was in America there was the Moravian John Cennick and John and Charles Wesley and many others, so why did he and other ministers from Wales need to accept invitations to preach over the border? He could preach in England because he was bilingual, but his English brothers in Christ were not able to preach in Welsh, which was the common language of the population in Wales. Only about ten per cent of Welsh people then could speak English.

John Wesley met Daniel Rowland at Llanmartin in October 1741 for a preaching tour. They both came to the Church at Machen, a village five miles east of Caerphilly, where they met Howell Harris and his companions. Rowland preached the first sermon in Welsh and John Wesley the second in English.

Daniel was a very honest man and did not seek to attract followers. He often encouraged his own countrymen not to come to Llangeitho, but to stay in their home parishes and preach the gospel, and teach in Societies.

Many people visited Llangeitho to hear Daniel Rowland and one Edward Morgan recorded his impressions:

> When he was engaged one Sunday morning [the monthly sacrament] in reading the church service his mind was more than usually occupied with the prayers; an unexpected overwhelming force came down upon his soul as he was praying in those melting evangelical words, 'By thine agony and bloody sweat, by thy cross and passion, by thy precious death and burial, by the coming of the Holy Spirit.' As he uttered these words a sudden amazing power seized his whole frame, and no sooner did seize him than it ran instantly like an electric shock through all the people in the church, so that many of them fell down on the ground. O how did the dying love of Christ affect them all, they mourned and wept as they looked unto the Lamb of God suffering for their sins.[1]

Daniel was not a lengthy preacher, rarely preaching for more than thirty to forty minutes, though on one memorable occasion he ended his sermon when the sun, he noticed, shone in at the west window. Four hours had passed, but no one was conscious of time; it seemed to some that eternity was very near. There was a tremendous power in all his preaching that quite overwhelmed his hearers.

The Reverend John Williams, of Dolyddelen (Snowdonia), walked to Llangeitho, and was so tired at the end of his journey that he ought to have gone to bed, rather than to chapel. However, he went to hear Rowland, who preached on Isaiah 25:6:

> And in this mountain shall the Lord of hosts make unto all people a feast of fat things, a feast of wines on the lees, of fat things full of marrow, of wines on the lees well refined. You never heard such a thing in your life. He began to tap the barrels of the covenant of grace and to let out the wine well refined and to give it to the people to drink. It flowed over the chapel. I also drank and became, as I may say, quite drunk [spiritually]. And there I was, and scores of others, in an ecstasy of delight, praising God, having forgotten all fatigue and bodily wants.

This account may sound a little poetic, but it shows how his preaching gripped the minds and hearts of his hearers. Others said he delivered his sermons 'with a passionate, and pathetic eloquence and red-hot earnestness'.

Howell Harris was now an itinerant preacher and he met Rowland unexpectedly for the first time at Defynnog, Breconshire, in August 1737. Afterwards Howell wrote of him:

> Upon hearing the sermon, and seeing the gifts given him and the amazing power and authority with which he spoke, and the effects it had on the people, I was made indeed thankful, and my heart burned with love to God and him.

This was indeed praise from a man who was considered to be one of the greatest preachers in Wales. Two years later he could report:

> There is a great revival in Cardiganshire, through Daniel Rowland, a Church minister, who has been much owned and blessed in Carmarthenshire also.

By the following year both Rowland and Harris were reporting the blessing that was following their preaching in South Wales; in the north it was more difficult as the opposition was greater. They both knew the power given to them in their preaching was from God, and they gazed with awe on the multitudes that came under conviction of sin. Even those that had been against their preaching and sceptical about its results came to hear and believe the gospel.

The English preacher George Whitefield, so greatly used by God in the British Isles and North America, on a few occasions shared the ministry with Daniel Rowland. He too was amazed at the authority and power that accompanied his preaching:

> The power of God at the Sacrament during the administration by Mr. Rowland was enough to make a person's heart burn within him.

David Jones of Llangan in South Wales was being asked to evaluate the difference between Whitefield and Rowland as preachers. In his reply he said:

> As regards the oratory, as regards the delivery, as regards the act of preaching, as regards the soaring to the heights and the lifting up of the congregation to the heavens I really could detect very little difference between them, it was this, that you could always be certain of getting a good sermon from Rowland, but not always from Whitfield.

**Note:**

1. Electricity had been discovered by the Ancient Greeks. In the eighteenth century it was used for medical shock treatment. It would be another century before it was harnessed to bring light and heat, displacing the use of candles and oil to light homes.

# CHAPTER 11

## SANCTIFIED ADVERSITY CARRIES THE RICHEST PEARL IN ITS MOUTH

*'I will be glad and rejoice in Your mercy, For You have considered
  my trouble;*
*You have known my soul in adversities.'*

Psalm 31:7

Daniel Rowland and Eleanor Davies married in 1734 during the period of Daniel's life-changing experience at Llanddewi-Brefi under Griffith Jones' ministry. Their marriage was a love match. No young lady would leave the congregation of Dissenters in which her family were fully committed to marry an Anglican cleric who was considered by the establishment to have gone mad. Because of their poor circumstances, for the first year of their marriage they lived at Caerllugest with his in-laws. She was a very faithful and loyal wife, supporting him to the end of her life. It must have been particularly hard providing for their three sons, John, Nathaniel and David, and four daughters when Daniel was on a curate's meagre stipend of £10 per annum. John, eldest son of Eleanor and Daniel, was born according to a note on the flyleaf of a Latin commentary of St Matthew (found at Caerllugest) at seven o'clock on Tuesday 14 October 1735 (no weight given!). As they held their baby son, Daniel and Eleanor could not have realised how as a young man he would be given authority over his father.

Daniel Rowland, like his contemporaries George Whitefield

and John and Charles Wesley, was a loyal ordained minister of the Church of England; but like the Sadducees and Pharisees of Our Lord's earthly ministry the bishops of the diocese were displeased with his preaching – especially on the subjects of free grace, the blood of Christ shed on the Cross for atonement, and the need for repentance and a personal faith in the Lord Jesus Christ. Often the bishops of the diocese of St David's had their opinion swayed by false stories and accusations that were conjured up by Rowland's enemies. Daniel Rowland and his companions in the gospel were slandered, despised, belittled and threatened. Rowland was a marked man and his enemies, like those who sought Christ's death, only waited for their moment of opportunity to bring his ministry to an end – so they hoped. This window of opportunity would come many years later.

Disaster struck the Rowland family when Daniel's brother John, Rector of Llangeitho, was drowned off Aberystwyth on 5 July 1760. Daniel had been his curate for twenty-five years. The Bishop of St David's instituted Daniel Rowland's son, also a John, as the new Rector of Llangeitho – a sure sign of the Bishop's displeasure at his father's ministry. This move by the Bishop, who knew of Daniel's bereavement, was a callous act. On his deathbed the Bishop was reported to have been greatly troubled in his mind. However, the new rector, John Rowland, did not stay long in residence. John Rowland, like so many of his generation, aspired to a better living with greater income. John found a curacy in the church of St Giles, Shrewsbury, Shropshire. A plaque in that church shows he married Mary, daughter of the Reverend William Gorsuch, and was a master at the free school in the town. So John Rowland, Daniel Rowland's eldest son, lived comfortably in the town with his wife and son (William Gorsuch Rowland, born 1770) for about fifty-five years. John was also curate of Clive – a small chapel in the parish of St Mary, Shrewsbury. These curacies supplemented his income from the living of Llangeitho until his death on 16 November 1815, aged eighty.

With the departure of the rector, John Rowland, to

Shrewsbury, the enemies of Daniel Rowland, curate at Llanddewi-Brefi, found their window of opportunity to silence his preaching. Whether John Rowland took any interest in his Welsh parish or came to the defence of his father we shall never know. Sometime in 1763 a notice revoking his licence was served without warning, but perhaps not unexpectedly, on Daniel in Llanddewi-Brefi Church by the Bishop of St David's, Nicholas Claggett – a disgrace for any minister of the Established Church and only served for exceptionally disgraceful misconduct. Daniel was only his son's curate there and no record was kept in the diocese of this unkindly act. Daniel did not deserve this kind of treatment from another member of the Church. This revocation was delivered by two clergymen who rudely interrupted the service while he was about to give the sermon. It is recorded that Daniel was heartbroken and shed tears of anguish during this event. His congregation followed him outside and encouraged him to continue the service and preach his sermon in the churchyard standing on the wall. Twenty-eight years earlier this was the place where Daniel was deeply awakened to his spiritual need by Griffith Jones. Events had turned full circle for Daniel. An eye-witness account states that when preaching at Nantcwmlle on the same day, where Daniel served as a curate under his son, Daniel was approached by two clerics who delivered a similar letter from the Bishop of St David's. No doubt the Bishop intended that his letter should be delivered at every parish under Daniel's charge. The Reverend William Williams[1] (not the famous hymn writer) was appointed Daniel's successor at Llangeitho.

The parish records of Nantcwmlle show that Daniel baptised Esther, daughter of John Morgan of Cilpyll, on 10 March 1770, even though he was barred from preaching there.

The history of the Christian Church has shown that those who are faithful in preaching the gospel to many thousands can expect persecution from within the Church as well as from without. Despite this, Daniel never held ill will against the Established Church and had the greatest respect for her, saying, 'There is a spark in the Prayer Book which will never be put out. Though it is hidden now, yet you may live to see it bursting out into bright flame.' Irreparable damage had been done to the Established Church in Wales. Bishop J. C. Ryle wrote, 'As long as the world stands the Church of England will never get over the injury done to it by the preposterous and stupid revocation of Daniel Rowland's licence.' Despite an attempt to have him reinstated by the churchwardens of the parish of Nantcwmlle, the Bishop angrily refused. Another attempt was made nine years after his ejection by John Thornton, one of the evangelical Clapham sect and patron of the parish of Newport, Pembrokeshire, who offered him the living in 1769. By this time Daniel knew no leading from his Master to leave Llangeitho.

Daniel's dismissal (they all, bar one, left with him) from the Church of England gave him a new freedom in his ministry, but this was not without extreme hardship to him and his family. "Oh! sanctified adversity carries the richest pearl in its mouth; it makes sin odious to us, but the return of the Saviour's presence doubly sweet!" was Daniel's comment on the suffering of the believer when preaching on Psalm 65 verse 5. Preaching on Psalm 66 verses 11–12, Daniel said, "We went through fire and water . . . there can be no gold or silver without being first purified by fire." During these difficult times Daniel was faithfully supported and encouraged in his ministry by his wife Eleanor (née Davies), who was descended from good Puritan stock. Her family were Dissenters and were members of the Cilgwyn group of churches. Her brother Peter married Magdalen Jones, who was related to Jenkin Jones, co-pastor with David Edwards of the Free Church in Abermeurig. These independent Churches met in their members' homes. Eleanor's sister-in-law Mary married Timothy Davis, who also led the flock at the Cilgwyn churches. So Eleanor and Daniel were surrounded by a family of Nonconformists!

It is very sad to write that because of the Bishop's action Holy Communion was not celebrated again at St Ceitho, Llangeitho Parish Church, during Daniel's life because the congregation only comprised one person. The Book of Common Prayer states, 'There shall be no celebrations of the Lord's Supper, except there be a convenient number to communicate with the Priest, according to his discretion.' After his expulsion a little meeting house that was aptly called Ty Seiet (House of Fellowship), which had been built in 1760 for the purpose of teaching on week nights and Saturdays, was his new 'parish centre'. A parcel of land was given to the evicted congregation by Eleanor's brother Peter Davies for a chapel in the adjoining village of Gwynfil. This chapel was rebuilt in 1764 when it became necessary due to the revival that followed soon after Daniel had his licence revoked. It was from there he preached until his death, assisted by his son Nathaniel, who was converted during the height of the revival in 1762. Unfortunately Peter Davies died returning home from Hereford two years after the chapel was completed. He was only forty-one years of age. He had been a widower since his wife Magdalen's death at the age of just thirty-six. Peter's mother died from a road accident returning from visiting her daughter Mary on the road near Cellan Church. Road accidents are not the stuff of the twenty-first century alone. The roads were terrible, and accidents happened when horses stumbled or carts and carriages overturned, often in terrible weather conditions. The Countess Lady Huntington and George Whitefield complained of the state of Welsh roads. Turnpike roads that were maintained were unpopular because of the charges made to travel over them, and this was the cause of the Rebecca Riots. It should remind us how protected were our three men, who travelled thousands of miles on what were no more than dirt tracks, and potholes were filled with stones and bricks that were themselves a danger.

Today the visitor to Llangeitho will see the little parish church with its white-painted wall surrounding the graveyard. The New Church site is only a quarter of a mile from the parish church where three generations of Rowlands had preached the gospel. The chapel on the site today has its own story to tell about the former building. If that chapel could speak it would have much to say about how the New Church came into being and the events that were to give Daniel a far greater ministry.

After his expulsion, the New Church became the centre of his preaching, and 2,000 and more attended each Saturday at noon for his teaching ministry. Regularly it was estimated that between twelve and fifteen thousand would come to hear the preacher at the monthly sacrament service and a pulpit was erected in the open air or he preached from an open window.

**Note:**

1. I use the name the Reverend William Williams (he was known as curate when he took up his curacy at St Geitho's on 5 August 1763) although his name in the diocese subscription book is shown as John Williams. The diocese subscription book is signed by the appointee to show he subscribes to royal supremacy, use of the Book of Common Prayer and adherence to the Thirty-nine Articles.

# CHAPTER 12

# THIS IS MY BODY BROKEN FOR YOU

*'This cup is the new covenant in My blood. This do, as often as you drink it, in remembrance of Me.'*

1 Corinthians 11:25

The first Sunday of each month became known as 'sacrament Sunday'. This was preceded on Saturday with a service in preparation for this remembrance that Jesus Christ had commanded his disciples to keep.

Derek Swann in the *Evangelical Library Bulletin* (Spring 1959) quoted from various sources concerning the preaching of Rowland:

> Soon Llangeitho began to attract people like moths to the light of a candle. The candle of the Lord had been set up and sinners were drawn to its light and warmth. On Communion Sundays at Llangeitho thousands came to hear the Word and receive the sacrament. Distance was no hindrance: on one occasion forty-five people set out from Caernarvon in the north, sailing as far as Aberystwyth and walking from there to Llangeitho. On the Monday they intended to go back in the same manner, but owing to high winds the ship did not sail, so they walked the whole distance. One old saint used to start out on Saturday night for Llangeitho and arrive in the early hours of Sunday morning. After a short sleep in a hay loft he went straight to the services. The Word was so powerfully preached by Mr. Rowland that all signs of tiredness were swept away, and the old man was heard to cry out early under [the influence of the] sermon, *'Blessed be God, I am already well paid. O the riches of Christ.'* Groups from Wrexham walked over the mountains of Montgomeryshire to receive fresh

supplies of the bread of life. People walked from Bala, from sixty miles away, and one lady who undertook this journey said that it would be worth while travelling from America to hear Daniel Rowland at Llangeitho.

George Whitefield made this observation:

> At seven in the morning I have seen perhaps ten thousand from different parts, in midst of the sermon crying glory and blessing, ready to leap for joy.

Those preaching during the revival were aware that the message of the gospel produced phenomena such as 'jumping' (for joy), tears and spontaneous outbursts of praise. Daniel preferred that his preaching should bring this reaction than one of sleep. William Williams of Pant-y-Celyn wrote in his elegy on Daniel Rowland's death, concerning his preaching:

> After preaching Sinai's thunder for a period without stay, there came a beautiful calm, a melting power, remarkable for its sweetness, which calmed the troubled breast. The deep groans, the great distress, gave place to ecstatic joy and shouts of praise. The sighs and scenes of horror gave place to shouts of *Diolch iddo, Gogoniaut, Bendigedig.* [Glory! Hallelujah! Thank God!]

Daniel believed passionately that the Holy Spirit brought the Word of God to life. He wrote to George Whitefield of this work of the Holy Spirit:

> Never before did I feel such power given me in preaching and administering the Lord's supper. The Lord comes down among us in such a manner as words cannot describe. Though I have to prevent nature mixing with work, openly discountenanced all crying out, God gives such light and power in the ordinance, that many cannot possibly help crying out, praising and adoring Jesus, being swallowed up in God, and this I was obliged to leave my whole congregation, being hundreds in a flame. . . . This is our condition generally every Sabbath.

At least eight or more well-respected ordained clergymen were privileged to assist Rowland in officiating at the Lord's Supper. This was so necessary as the number of communicants was immense.

In his letter dated 1 March 1743 Howell Harris wrote to George Whitefield:

> Last Sunday, I was with brother Rowland at the ordinance, where I saw, heard, and felt such things as I cannot communicate on paper. I never before witnessed such crying, heart-breaking groans, silent weeping, holy mourning and shouts of joy and rejoicing. Their 'Amens' and crying of 'glory to God in the highest' would have inflamed your soul had you been there. It is very common, when Rowland preaches, for scores to fall down by the power of the Word. Some are there for hours, some praising and admiring Jesus Christ and free grace, others wanting words to express their feelings. Mr. Rowland's congregation consists of above 2000 people, the greater part brought into Glorious liberty. O my brother my heart is full. I am sure God is about to do a work in Wales. Revival is everywhere.

Christmas Evans a well-known preacher, gives an eye-witness account of one of the services at the New Church, Llangeitho (this does not appear to have been a sacrament service). He shows vividly the preaching of Rowland. He likens the content and delivery of the sermon to opening boxes of fragrant perfume. We know that there were no pews, so people stood; the language was Welsh; and sometime after the service commenced Rowland, wearing his black gown, would enter the pulpit through a small door behind the elevated pulpit. It will be later explained why he made his entry in this way. It certainly was not for effect – there was a worthier motive. The following is an extract from his account:

> It was the general practice for an [ordained] minister to read and pray before Rowland made his appearance in the pulpit. He then frequently gave out with a clear and audible voice that stanza in Psalm 27:4 to be sung: *One thing have I desired of the Lord, that will I seek after*. . . . Only one verse was sung before the sermon in those days notable for divine influences. The whole congregation joined in singing the stanza with great fervour, yet repeating it but a few times before the sermon, lest the heavenly

ointment would run over the vessels too soon. Then Rowland would stand up and read his text distinctly to the hearing of all. The whole congregation were all ears and most attentive, as if they were on the point of hearing some evangelic and heavenly oracle. And the eyes of all the people were at the same time most intensely fixed upon him. He had, at the commencement of his discourse, some stirring, striking idea, as a small box of ointment which he opened before the great one in his sermon, and it filled all the house with its heavenly perfume, as the odour of Mary's alabaster box of ointment at Bethany formerly; the congregation being delightfully enlivened with the sweet odour, were prepared to look for more of it from one box after the other throughout the sermon. Having thus roused the congregation with some uncommon thought, he would divide his text, and then proceed with the first division, bending his head down a little, as if to glance at his notes, on a piece of paper before him.

Now we are coming to the most difficult part of the description, because we cannot make a dumb image speak, or a dead man live. I will however borrow another similitude, in order to give some idea of the manner of his most energetic eloquence. It shall be taken from the trade of a blacksmith. The smith first puts the iron into the fire, then blows the bellows softly, making some enquiries respecting the work to be done, the horse-shoes to be made, the plough-shares to be steeled, and the coulters to be repaired: but his eye during all that time is fixed steadily upon the process of heating the iron in the fire; as soon as he perceives it to be in a proper and pliable state, he carries it to the anvil and brings the weighty hammer or sledge down on the metal, and, in the midst of stunning noise and fiery sparks, emitted from the glowing metal, he fashions and moulds it at his will. Thus Rowland, having glanced at his notes as a matter of form, would go on with his discourse in a calm and deliberate manner, speaking with a free and audible voice; but he would gradually become warmed with his subject, and his voice became at length so elevated and authoritative, that it resounded through the whole chapel! The effect on the people was wonderful; you could see nothing but smiles, and tears running down the faces of all the people. Joyful exclamations were at the same time uttered by the vast assembly. And all this arose from the flame of his voice and the grandeur of his matter; and his animation arose from the flame that was in the sublime thoughts which he delivered. This first flame of heavenly devotion, under the first division, having subsided, he would again look on his scrap of notes, and commence the second time to melt and to make the minds of the people supple, until he formed them again unto the same heavenly temper. And thus he acted six or even seven times, as some say, in the same sermon. Rowland's voice, countenance, and appearance, used to change exceedingly in the pulpit, and he seemed to be greatly excited; but there was nothing low or disagreeable in him, all was becoming, dignified, and excellent. There was such a vehement invincible flame in his ministry as effectually dispelled and drove away the careless, worldly, dead spirit: and the people, so awakened, drew nigh, as it were in the bright cloud, to Christ, and to Moses and Elijah. Eternity and its amazing realities were rushing into their minds!

There was very little if any inference or application at the end of Rowland's sermon, for he had been applying and enforcing the glorious truths of the gospel throughout the whole of his discourse. He would conclude with a very few striking and forcible remarks, which were most overwhelming and invincible; and then he would make a very sweet short prayer, and utter the benediction. Then he would, full of perspiration; make haste out of the pulpit through the little door. His exit was as sudden as his entrance.

The Reverend William Williams of Crickhowell has described the outset of revival in the churches in the period that this book covers:

Those revivals usually occurred, not as the result of any predetermined and special effort to produce them, but in the ordinary means of grace, and were frequently unexpected by the great mass of the congregation. As it was on the day of Pentecost, when the disciples, 'were all with one accord in one place, suddenly there came a sound from heaven as of a mighty rushing wind, and it filled all the house where they were sitting,' it has often happened in Wales. When the congregation had assembled together to hold the usual service, and while that service was proceeding in the usually quiet manner, the preacher would suddenly find himself under some unusual influence – felt at liberty to relinquish the string of his discourse, and to utter words which were not on his paper, and thoughts which had not occurred to him in his study. Some of the oldest brethren and sisters would soon recognize the sound. John would remark to his brother Simon, 'It is the Lord!' and possibly follow the glad announcement with the shout, *'Gogoniant!'* [glory] to which Simon would respond with, *'Diolch iddo byth!'* [Praise to God, who has remembered]. Presently the whole congregation was ablaze. Christians shouted for joy that their good Lord had again visited them, while numbers who had been so far indifferent to their souls' salvation would send forth the distressing cry, 'What shall we do to be saved?'

It was no transient feeling. It would be present at the next service, and the next afterwards, and for months to come. It would spread to the adjoining districts, perhaps over the whole country, and possibly over the greater part of Wales.

William Williams of Crickhowell, whom we already have quoted, answered the critics who attributed the manifestations to excitement:

There were remarks made on the Revival, in the days of Daniel Rowland, equally wise, enlightened, and intellectual with those which are made in the present day. It is easy to say that 'it was all excitement.' There was excitement, we admit, and much of it; but we scarcely believe that there is any one prepared to say that there was none on the day of Pentecost. But to say that it was all excitement is quite another matter, if by that it is intended to imply that it was a momentary feeling, which passed away without leaving any lasting beneficial effect on those who experienced it. There is abundant and conclusive evidence in thousands of instances, that that idea is quite a mistaken one. There may be different opinions as to the propriety of those manifestations. The Rev. Rowland Hill, during one of his visits into Wales, witnessed some of these scenes, and said, 'I like the fire; but don't like the smoke.' It was prettily said, and quite in character with many of the other sayings of that eminent man; but perhaps it would have been too difficult, under the circumstances of the time, to get the one without the other. It is possible that the people allowed themselves to be too much excited, – that they ought not to have shouted, and that it was very blameworthy in them to jump. We are not at all disposed to argue that point; but it is certain that thousands of those who were thus excited, and who expressed their feelings in cries of distress, and in shouts of gratitude, underwent at the time the great change, and proved themselves for the remainder of their lives to be new creatures.

Daniel likened revival to a 'heath fire' that we know may smoulder for many days before it is fanned into flames by the wind.

Howell Harris, who had been preaching often to thousands, sometimes several times a day, and who was considered by many to the be the 'herald' of the revival, heard Daniel Rowland preach on Proverbs 8: 32: 'Now therefore hearken unto me, O you children: blessed are those who keep my ways.' This sermon had a dramatic and lasting impact on Harris. He now understood in his innermost soul how Christ was pleading at the throne of Grace for him, and he was now willing to surrender all to him. He now knew how great Christ's love was for him, and that all that Christ had done was a sure and secure foundation for his eternal salvation. This text, the early Church fathers interpreted as referring to Christ (Christological interpretation), with its personification of Wisdom. From Harris's words we gather this was the interpretation that Daniel applied on that day, giving Christ the central place in his message. He found Christ in all the scriptures, not just in the New Testament. Like the apostle Paul, Daniel knew the great truth contained in the text 'Christ the power of God and the wisdom of God' (1 Corinthians 1:24). He had seen the truth in this text working experientially in the deliverance of himself, his flock and his wider audience from sin, hell and the Devil.

Many more, like Harris, came under Rowland's preaching, had Christ's atoning work dramatically personalised in their lives, and were ever thankful that God had spoken to them through the 'prophet' from Llangeitho. Rowland to thousands was not just a great preacher – he was far more than that. He was in a sense an *apostolic figure* sent by God for these times of refreshing. When the spirit of revival moved through the exiles that had returned from captivity and had just completed rebuilding the foundation of the Lord's temple some shouted for joy and others wept. Ezra recorded the event (Ezra 3:12–13):

Many of the priests and Levites and heads of the fathers' houses, old men who had seen the first temple, wept with a loud voice when the foundation of this temple was laid before their eyes. Yet many shouted for joy, so the people could not discern the noise of the shout of joy from the noise of weeping of the people.

Surely this is what happened during the revival in Wales.

# CHAPTER 13

## THE PRICE AND POWER OF REVIVAL

*'And when He had sent the multitudes away, He went up on the mountain by Himself to pray. Now when the evening came, He was alone there.'*

Matthew 14:23

There is no secret as to why Daniel's ministry was so blessed; the explanation is quite simple. His relationship with God was at its heart. Jesus Christ was not only his Saviour but his *Lord*. Nothing was to be allowed to intrude into that close harmony. He knew that his ministry to his flock and his energetic zeal of proclaiming the gospel throughout Wales was dependent on that relationship being untainted by any unwanted intrusion. He did not rely on his natural or spiritual gifts, but his reliance was on his saviour alone. He could not preach a sermon without knowing that its substance was from God and that it would be energised by the Holy Spirit. He wrestled with God in prayer for his congregation; he wanted them to hear, not *his* words, but words that were delivered with the unction of the Holy Spirit.

Before he preached in any church he would want to be alone with God. He had learned from his saviour that it was necessary to be alone with his heavenly Father. He interceded for his hearers as well as for himself; he took hours in prayer over his responsibility for proclaiming the Gospel publicly.

He would rise at four in the morning and eat breakfast, and then he would spend the next hours in the company of his

Saviour. He would often go into solitary places, such as woods or hills, meditating on the sermon he would give a few hours later. He filled his mind with what he believed God would have him say to his congregation. He had strong feelings and wanted the Holy Spirit to take control of these while he was preaching. He wanted no matter, however important, to come between this time of fellowship and the moment he was in the pulpit. Now his mind and whole being was ready to deliver the message that God had laid on his heart for his people. This is why he entered the pulpit during the service. He left the house next to the New Church at Llangeitho and silently climbed the steps outside behind the chapel as the congregation was singing and entered through the small door into the pulpit thoroughly prepared to preach.

His entrance was occasionally late. Once the convener of the service found him still in bed, and Daniel protested that God had not given him the message to be delivered to the large congregation that was already arriving. The convener was a very good and faithful friend who with words of wisdom encouraged him to prepare for the service. He climbed the steps and entered the pulpit to give a most challenging and powerful sermon. On another occasion the convener of the service was concerned that Daniel Rowland had not entered the pulpit, so a messenger was sent to find him. On arriving at his study door he could hear Rowland saying, "I can't go without You. Unless You come with me I cannot go." The messenger reported back telling the convener that he did not hear with what words the other person had replied! The convener, however, realised that Rowland was pleading with the Lord. He arrived in the pulpit shortly after the messenger had returned, and after preaching he left by the same door. There was a good reason for this exit: during the service he had lost much energy in the chapel, which became very hot, and he was perspiring profusely. He went home to change into a dry shirt!

Daniel was a pastor and prayed earnestly for his people often with tears. He would ride up into the hills around Llangeitho and look down on the farms and hamlets; he knew each person and prayed for them. At the beginning of his ministry he lamented over their homes not being places of prayer, but later was thankful to God when he saw the fruits of his ministry. Now he could see homes of prayer and families who worshipped together in their homes before beginning their daily work. He was a shepherd who loved his flock. He knew the Great Revival had not started with him or in a public service of worship, but in several families meeting together in the neighbourhood of Llangeitho. These brethren worshipped God daily with their own households, and there they experienced the gracious work of the Holy Spirit descending upon their souls. As they prayed, they emptied themselves of all inappropriate motives and they became the vehicles of God's amazing power. There they experienced the divine fire carrying the flame to the New Church, where it became a blaze which spread far and wide through the mountains and valleys of the surrounding country. Time and time again revival in the Church has come this way irrespective of culture or denomination. *Their homes were the birthplace of revival.*

One has only to read about the lives of those who ministered during later revivals to learn that they followed the Lord's practice of prayer. The Reverend Douglas Brown[1], who was called from South-West London to minister during the East Anglian revival in 1921, and the Reverend Duncan Campbell, who was called to minister in the Hebrides during the time of revival in 1949, both spent much time alone in prayer. Duncan Campbell would say, "Give the best hours of the day to God." He had taken note of the few words on the flyleaf of Dr Stuart Holden's Bible written by his mother:

> Begin the day with God. See His face first, before you see the face of another.[2]

Douglas Brown dearly loved his people at Ramsden Road Baptist Church, Balham, London, and shed tears when God called him to leave them for East Anglia and then to become an itinerant preacher and convention speaker. These men, like

Daniel, had a heart for their people and knew the power of prayer born out of a deep relationship with God.

It is appropriate to refer again to Duncan Campbell; in his sermon on Acts 4:29–31 he challenged his listeners to consider the price of revival:

> Revival is not going to come merely by attending conferences or conventions, though that may contribute to it. When 'Zion travailed she brought forth children'. Oh, may God bring us there, may God lead us through to the place of absolute surrender. I shall never forget that dear saint of God, Dr. Inwood, cry at the 1924 Keswick Convention, 'Christian men and women, <u>self-renunciation is the cardinal ethic of the Christian Church</u>.' Is it not true, too often our very best moments of yielding and consecration are mingled with the destructive element of self-preservation? A full and complete surrender is the price of blessing, but that also *is the price of revival*.[3]

Only thirteen of Daniel's sermons out of thousands he gave were translated into English. They are well worth reading. Each sermon shows his evangelistic zeal and his knowledge of God's Word. He preached of the need for repentance for the enormity of sin, and for faith in Christ's blood shed for sinners on the Cross. It is no wonder that strong men broke down and wept when they heard the gospel, or that they uttered cries of praise when they came into full assurance of faith. Here were men, women and children who knew deep in their souls they were held guilty by God, but found forgiveness at the Cross. No doubt a chorus of hallelujahs was raised in heaven! On his last Sunday in the chapel, Daniel had been very unwell in the preceding days; he knew as he wearily climbed the steps that it was his last day there. Entering the pulpit he said:

> I am almost leaving, and am on the point of being taken from you. I am not tired of the work, but in it. I believe that my heavenly Father will soon release me from my labours and bring me to my everlasting rest, but I hope He will continue His gracious presence with you after I am gone. . . . I have nothing

to say about my acceptance with God but what I have said at all times, I die as a poor sinner, resting solely and altogether upon the merits of a crucified Saviour.

His request was granted by God. He passed into glory a few days later on Saturday 16 October 1790. He was buried in a grave next to his granddaughter Jennet (who died aged ten in 1784) by Llangeitho Parish Church, where he had served as curate under his brother and son. At the graveside two sermons were given. David Jones of Llangan preached to the assembled crowds on Revelation 14:13 – 'I heard a voice from heaven saying to me, 'Write blessed are the dead which die in the Lord from henceforth: Yes, said the Spirit, they may rest from their labours; and their works do follow them.' John Williams preached on 2 Timothy 4:8 – 'Henceforth there is laid up for me a crown of righteousness, which the Lord the righteous judge shall give me at that day; and not to me only, but unto all them also that love his appearing.' Eleanor passed to be with her Lord a few months later, on 9 August 1792.

Possibly by divine providence, on the reordering of the parish church at Llangeitho Daniel's grave was brought under the chancel, where it is marked by a commemorative tablet.

Daniel was a self-effacing man, who only once consented to sit for his portrait. Robert Bowyer was commissioned for this work by Lady Huntingdon, who was generous with her money, which perhaps could have been better spent. No wonder she died leaving debts! The portrait once hung in the parish church at Llangeitho, where he served as a curate and from which he was prevented from preaching after his licence revocation was delivered to him at Llanddewi-Brefi. The portrait now hangs in the National Library of Wales.

Chapel Gwynfil, built in 1813, replaced the New Church on the same site that had been built for Rowland when he was drawing the crowds. On an autumn morning in 1883 anyone passing Chapel Gwynfil was to behold a strange sight. Among a crowd gathered round something covered by a white sheet were Dr Lewis Edwards and the Reverend Thomas Levi of

Aberystwyth, Moderator of the Calvinistic Methodist General Assembly. Dr Edwards pulled a cord revealing a white marble statue, almost life-size, of Daniel Rowland. It was placed on the very spot once occupied by the New Church. The Reverend Levi, who was leading the event, had raised £600 so that Edward Griffith of Chester could fashion this near likeness. The Reverend Levi was responsible for erecting monuments to William Williams of Pant-y-celyn; to Bishop Morgan, translator of the Bible into Welsh; and to our third link in the Glorious Chain – Thomas Charles. Daniel certainly would be affronted by this statue of himself erected 150 years after his ordination, but he was not there to argue; he was in a better place, enjoying the loving welcome from his Lord: "Well done, My faithful servant."

What makes the attendance figures at Llangeitho over so many years so amazing? If you look at a map of Wales and see the geographical position of Llangeitho, you will notice that it is many miles from any large town. Llangeitho, then a small village of no more than 300 inhabitants, was certainly not a likely place to find a minister with a weekly congregation of 2,000! Rowland's regular congregation came from hamlets and villages where people had been deeply affected by his ministry, and they became disciples of Christ, spreading the good news. They came from all walks of life and all classes of society. Because of the tremendous impact of Griffith Jones' circulating schools a high proportion were literate and therefore well educated judged by the standards of their day; they were also eager to learn more about their faith. Very few owned Bibles, because of the expense, and even if they could afford a copy none were easily available. They were spiritually fed by hearing the great preachers and by gathering together in the Methodist Societies where they were nurtured; the Societies that Howell Harris and his co-workers founded, supervised and promoted were training grounds for potential pastors, preachers, evangelists and teachers. The work of the revival in Wales was essentially one of the Holy Spirit; it cannot be accounted for by the actions of men alone, however gifted they may have been.

Owing to the conversions through his preaching and that of his friends there was a growing band of men who would swell the numbers of preachers. They would eventually be ordained and would continue the work of God well into the next century. The greatest need, though, was for Bibles in the Welsh language.

**Notes:**

1. Read about Douglas Brown in *A Forgotten Revival* by Stanley C. Griffin, DayOne, Epson, 1992.

2. *Channel of Revival*, a biography of Duncan Campbell by Andrew A. Woolsey, The Faith Mission, Edinburgh, 1974, page 156.

3. Op. cit.

*Portrait of Daniel Rowland.*

*Statue of Daniel Rowland.*

*St Ceitho Parish Church, Llangeitho, Ceredigion.*

*Gwynfil Chapel,  Llangeitho.*

*Gwynfil Chapel, Llangeitho, interior, kindly supplied by Eirian Jones, Secretary and Deacon of Gwynfil Chapel.*

*Parish Church, Llandewi-Brefi.*

*Daniel Rowland's catechism.*

# CHAPTER 14

# THOMAS CHARLES, TO WHOM MILLIONS SHOULD BE THANKFUL

*'Let no one despise your youth, but be an example to the believers in word, in conduct, in love, in spirit, in faith, in purity.'*
1 Timothy 4:12.

Thomas Charles was a son of Rice Charles, a farmer, and his wife, Jael, in the parish of Llanfihangel Abercynwyn. This hamlet is situated two miles north of Laugharne on the River Taf, south-west of St Clears, Carmarthen. Thomas was born at Longmoor Farm on Tuesday 14 October 1755. Soon after his birth the family moved to Pant Dwfn, in the same parish.

Jael was the daughter of influential landowner David Bowen, and the Charles family lived comfortably off the income from the farm. This was Rice's second marriage. His first wife, Jane, died after giving birth to their daughter Sage; they had a son William born in October 1739. By his second marriage Rice had other children and they worshipped at Llanfihangel Abercywyn Church with their five daughters and five sons, plus six servants. They were a fairly wealthy family and able to educate their children, which included sending Thomas to Carmarthen Academy. They took Communion from a silver chalice reputed to be 300 years old and inscribed, 'POCVLYM + ECLESLAE + DE + LLANVICHANGELL + ABERCOWEN'. During this time Rice Charles had increased the land he farmed to 367 acres. Today the church at Llanfihangel Abercynwyn is a pile of stones because when a new church was built further to the east in more recent times the old one was left to decay.

From the age of ten Thomas was sent to a school at Llanddowror founded by Griffith Jones. Other pupils who passed through this school were Howell Harris, the great preacher, William Williams of Pant-y-celyn, the hymn writer, and Peter Williams, another fine pastor and preacher. Rice Charles sent his son to the school as he wanted him to be a priest in the Church of England. Thomas spent four fruitful years at Griffith Jones' school. It was twenty years since Daniel Rowland had experienced the life-changing encounter with Griffith Jones at Llanddewi-Brefi; the old warrior for God had since been buried next to his wife, Margaret, at Llanddowror, but Madam Bridget Bevan was still administering the schools.

Thomas, during his schooldays, came under the influence of Rees Hugh, a holy man who was often filled with great joy. Thomas made sure to visit him once or twice a week and was greatly blessed by the influence of this godly man. Thomas wrote of him, 'I loved him as my father in Christ.' According to Thomas, Rees Hugh was an 'old disciple of Christ'.

During his time at school in Llanddowror, Thomas made a public profession of faith at his confirmation service. He showed his suitability to be a pastor as he was keen to influence his family and relatives towards spiritual matters, but how much he understood about the true nature of the gospel is questionable as he does not date his conversion to this time.

Thomas furthered his education at Carmarthen Academy at the age of fourteen. Like many teenagers he was in 'fear and dread' at the prospect of the change of school. His friend Rees Hugh was concerned for his well-being at the academy and prayed earnestly for him, resulting in Thomas being greatly blessed. God kept him away from careless and high-spirited students. While at the academy he went to hear the famous Reverend Daniel Rowland preach at the New Church, Llangeitho. That day, 20 January 1773, Rowland preached on the text from Hebrews 4:15 – 'For we have not an high priest which cannot be touched with the feelings of our infirmities; but was in all points tempted like as we are, yet without sin.' In his diary Thomas likened the change which took place in his mind to a 'blind man receiving sight'. Christ's love, compassion, power and sufficiency filled his soul with joy unspeakable. Until then Thomas had some idea of the gospel truths that he said were 'floating in my head, but they never powerfully and with divine energy penetrated my heart till now'. The truths expressed by Daniel Rowland seemed 'too wonderfully gracious to be true'. At the age of twenty he matriculated and entered Jesus College, Oxford, on 31 May 1775.

We cannot be sure who paid for his university education. His father was extending his farm with his increasing wealth, but finance did not come from that source; otherwise it would not have suddenly ceased without warning. His grandmother had left him a small gift in her will and this may have been contested. Thomas wrote about this crisis in his diary:

> About two years after I was entered I was brought into a very great strait and difficulty; my supplies from Wales were at once stopped, nor was there one resource to which I could look with any prospect of success this happened also when I was indebted to the college twenty pounds; things remained in this state for about a fortnight, during which time my mind was much distressed and perplexed, quite at a loss what to do. At last I resolved to inform the college how matters stood and went to go into the country to get my livelihood anyhow. I found my mind perfectly submissive to the Lord's will, and satisfied yet he should order all my concerns according to his own goodness and wisdom. But I was exceedingly puzzled to account for those concurring providences which opened my way thither, nor was I wholly without some secret trust yet the Lord would bring me through some way or other.

The £20 was the bond that an undergraduate had to place with the college as a contingency against student debt. It was likely that he had to draw upon this sum. So fees were a problem for students even in the eighteenth century!

Thomas kept his trust in God, and this was to be honoured by a visit from John Mayor, who was an undergraduate at Worcester College. John was a close friend of Thomas and they shared the same evangelical faith. All through their lives they were to care deeply for each other. Thomas shared his financial problems with

John, who assured him that he was not to worry. A few days later Thomas was invited to the home of William Fletcher, an Alderman of Oxford and a draper by trade. He was the son of James Fletcher, who was the owner of a bookshop highly valued by serious-minded undergraduates.

William was a successful businessman and a partner in the Old Bank; he was wealthy enough to help Thomas, who shared his evangelical faith through his days at Oxford, with a student loan. Thomas was able to pay off his debts and continue his studies without concern for his financial position. John Mayor had shown his concern for his friend in a tangible form, in finding funding from William Fletcher. John Mayor was to become Vicar of Shawbury, Shropshire, and John and Thomas remained close friends for the rest of their lives.

# CHAPTER 15

# ORDINATION AND A CURACY
# IN SOMERSET

*'Preach the word! Be ready in season and out of season. Convince, rebuke, exhort, with all longsuffering and teaching.'*

2 Timothy 4:2

During his latter days in Oxford, Thomas had applied for several curacies, but he declined those offered until he received a letter from his friend the Reverend Edward Griffin introducing him to the Reverend Henry Newman:

> A gentleman, a Clergyman in this neighbourhood [Leicestershire] his name Newman, about a twelvemonth past, has I trust experienced the Power of the Gospel of Christ, and from a persecutor, been made a preacher of it. In consequence of his change, he was expelled from his curacy, and received notice to quit his house. As he has two livings, in Somerset [Shepton Beauchamp and Sparkford], he proposes going there this summer to reside. He will want a curate and seems desirous to have you whom I mentioned to him; but he will not want you till Michaelmas.

The Reverend Henry Newman offered Thomas two rooms in his own house and use of his horse. This must have been a great inducement to be his curate, responsible for the parishes of Sparkford and Shepton Beauchamp, Somerset, but he soon found things were not to be easy!

Thomas was ordained deacon in the Church of England on Sunday 14 June 1778 at the Cathedral Church of Christ,

Oxford, by Bishop Dr John Butler. His first duty as curate was to officiate at the marriage of John Tucker of the Parish of Queen Camel to Mary Spooner of Sparkford, both in the county of Somerset, on 30 November 1778. At the close of the year he was able to write in his diary:

> It rejoices me yet my name is cast out as evil for the Lord's sake, I hope I am enabled to choose to suffer affliction with the people of God rather than the pleasure of sin for a season, all my desire is yet I may be enabled to fight the good fight, keep the faith and finish my course with joy and triumph.

Thomas was feeling a certain unease about his curacy in Sparkford and he was aware he was viewed with some hostility from the surrounding villages. There was real affliction to come in the next few months because of his evangelistic sermons. Shortly he was to move from his lodgings with his rector at Shepton Beauchamp to Mr Dove's at Queen Camel. This turned out to be a bad move. These Somerset villages he served were known for their rivalry, which often exhibited itself in unruly brawling and punch-ups. A neighbouring parish had recently sent their Welsh curate packing because they considered he was a Methodist, and those in Queen Camel, where he was now lodging, disliked their Presbyterian physician, Mr Dove, and called his new lodger a 'Methodist parson'. Thomas moved to be near his main charge, Sparkford, early in his curacy, so probably did not know of local rivalries. Thomas found himself isolated and he wrote to a fellow minister, 'I have no Christian friend to speak to within fifteen miles and Mr. Newman's unexpected behaviour has produced a coolness.' Obviously this small corner of Somerset had not welcomed the evangelical faith or the gospel preaching of their new curate and possibly their new vicar, Mr Newman.

His curacy under the Reverend Henry Newman was a difficult time. The final straw came when Mr Newman asked Thomas to take a twenty-five-per-cent cut in stipend or leave by Lady Day (25 March) 1779. This followed Mr Dove's notice to quit his lodgings. It is not surprising, therefore, because of the ill feeling from his boss and his parishioners, that he had to choose whether or not to leave his curacy after only a few months. It was difficult for him to take a cut of that magnitude as he had a responsibility to repay his student loan to Mr Fletcher in Oxford. Thomas was to take a cut in his pay although according to Mr Newman it was due to his own financial straits! Perhaps there were pressures put on Mr Newman from his parishioners. He possibly remembered his own circumstances in Leicester.

By the time the Reverend Henry Newman took up the living of Sparkford his patronage was with his eldest brother, Francis (Frank) Newman of South Cadbury. Frank Newman, a lawyer, had inherited the Sparkford and Cadbury estates from his uncle Francis Newman in 1764. Frank had got himself into financial and legal difficulties and in 1776 was found guilty of perverting the course of justice. He was sent to prison pending payment of heavy fines and securities. His name was also removed from the roll of Justices of the Peace. The biographer[1] of the Newman family describes Frank and his brother Charles as 'somewhat disreputable characters who brought the Newman name into disrepute'. So this was the situation in the Newman family when Thomas Charles arrived in Somerset to serve under the youngest brother, Henry, who had been converted while serving as a curate in Leicestershire.

Thomas found a good friend in the Reverend John Lucas[2], Rector of St John the Evangelist at Milborne Port, about eight miles away in Dorset. On his wise advice, Thomas decided to stay with his curacy at Sparkford. He was invited to assist John Lucas at Milborne Port from Monday 27 March 1780. The arrangement was that he should assist John Lucas for a few days each week, and in return Thomas would live with Mr Lucas, who would also provide him with a horse and pay him £10 a year to help him in his difficult financial circumstances. Thomas took priest's orders on 21 May 1780, and in September 1782 was presented with the perpetual curacy of South Barrow[3] by the Reverend John Hughes of St Denys.

While Thomas is our third link in this Glorious Chain, there were to be further links forged under his preaching; because of the great work he set in place by the founding of the Bible Society the number of links must be countless.

**Note:**

1. www.newmanfamilytree

2. The Reverend John Lucas died in office in 1785.

3. He gave up this curacy on 22 September 1790.

# CHAPTER 16

## AN ARDENT DESIRE AND A SECRET HOPE

*'Now Jacob loved Rachel; so he said, 'I will serve you seven years for Rachel your younger daughter.'*

Genesis 29:18

We must take a step back a few months; otherwise we shall miss an important event in the life of Thomas that was to change the course of his life and encourage him to return to Wales. After his graduation from Oxford and before taking up his curacy at Sparkford, because he was not required there until Michaelmas Thomas decided to accept an invitation to spend a summer holiday in Bala with his friend and fellow Oxford graduate Simon Lloyd. The Lloyds were a well-known family who lived at Plas yn Dre, Bala, a small town in Gwynedd. During this holiday Thomas was introduced to Sarah Jones, of whom he had already heard, and he had surprisingly set his affections on her although they had never met! He had heard about her from friends. There were no photographs in those days, but physical descriptions of her may have been given by friends. We are told that Sarah was beautiful and highly regarded for her Christian faith. Her fame went far beyond Bala and Thomas had heard of her six years before their first meeting, when he lived in Carmarthen. He had been attracted by what he learned, and he resolved one day to meet her. Sarah – or Sally, as she was called – lived with her mother and stepfather, Thomas Foulks, in Bala.

Sally was born to David and Sian Jones on Monday 12

November 1753; sadly her father died when she was about six years old. Thomas Foulks' first wife, Margaret, died in March 1759. We are not sure how Thomas Foulks and Sian Jones met, but it may have been through their Methodist Association in Bala. Sian was an early convert of Howell Harris. Thomas Foulks was converted to the Lord Jesus Christ through the preaching of John Wesley in Chester, where he was working as a carpenter. He joined the Wesleyan Methodists in Chester and continued to give financial support to them for the rest of his life. After her mother's marriage to Thomas Foulks, Sally loved him as her own father and must have prayed for him often as he went out preaching the gospel throughout Merioneth. As Sally grew up she took on the responsibility of the family business. She became a successful businesswoman in the town and often was away at markets selling lace and buying household goods. Sally worked for her parents; their shop contained everything for the home and personal wear. (This shop is now a branch of Barclays Banks PLC.) Her service to her parents allowed her stepfather, a Methodist, to continue preaching at weekends and during the week. When he was able he worked in the business, but Sally carried the brunt of the concerns and cares of the day-to-day management. Her stepfather and her mother depended heavily on her support.

In a letter Thomas wrote to Sally in 1779, after an interval of five months since their first meeting, he shared his belief that Sally was God's choice for him, to be his wife and companion in the gospel. However, there was a tension between his serving God in England and his desire to marry the woman he loved. Her family's dependence on her kept her in Bala, and his service in the Church kept him in England. His loyalty to his Lord and his service to the Church kept him from visiting her in Bala. Here is his first letter to Sally. It shows his deep love for this lovely Christian woman, who was then in her mid-twenties.

Rev Thomas Charles
Queen Camel
Near Sherborne
County of Dorset

My very dear friend,

Such an unexpected address from a person who never saw you but once, and that at such a long interval of time, will I suppose at first not a little surprise you: however I flatter myself that thus circumstanced it comes with the more recommendation, when I assure you that long as the interval is since I had the pleasure of seeing you, you have not been absent from my mind, for a whole day, from that time to this. The first report of your character (which I heard at Carmarthen by some of our religious friends about six years ago) left such an impression on my mind as, I am sure, no length of time can ever obliterate. I immediately conceived an ardent desire, and a secret hope, that my Heavenly Father's wise and good providence would so order subsequent events that I should in due time see that beloved person of whom I had formed such a favourable opinion. When Mr. Lloyd gave me a kind invitation to spend part of the summer with him at Bala, 'tis inexpressible what secret pleasure and joy the prospect of seeing you afforded me – Nor was I disappointed – The sight of so much good sense, beauty and unaffected modesty, joined with that genuine Piety which eminently adorns your person, administered Fuel to the Fire already enkindled, and which has continued burning with increasing ardour from that Time to this. I should then have explained to you what this letter informs you of, had not difficulties (then insurmountable) been in the way, originating from circumstances which I hope at some future period you'll give me leave to acquaint you with. Ever since I came to England I have anxiously expected (and not without some foundation, as assured by my friends) that some favourable circumstance would open a door for my return to Wales (a place for ever dear!) but hitherto I have been disappointed. Finding that any longer delay would serve only to distract my mind, and by constant uneasiness in some degree, unfit me for the proper discharge of that very important office in which I am engaged, I determined upon the resolution which I now put in execution, of writing to you, and solicit the favour of a correspondence with you till such Time as kind Providence indulges us with an interview, which on my part is most ardently desired. This favour I hope no impediment stands in the way preventing your granting it me all, but that of a previous engagement, I trust can easily be removed – Be perfectly assured that nothing but real regard and sincere affection for your person only, could ever induce me to write or speak to you on such a subject – You are the only person that ever I saw (and the first I ever addressed on the subject), with whom I thought I could spend my life in happy union and felicity, and for whom I possessed that particular affection and esteem requisite for conjugal happiness; and you are the only temporal blessing I have for some time past asked with importunity of the Lord – I hope that your determination will happily convince me that the Lord's answer is favourable – I shall be present with you when you pursue this, how anxious I shall be for your determination; 'tis impossible to tell how happy would I deem myself, could I be really present then to confirm to your full satisfaction what I assert in this letter! but as that at present is impossible, I hope to commit this, as well as all other events to Him, who rules supremely in the whole Universe, and orders all things in the best manner for the advancement of His own glory, and the Eternal welfare of His people, and no doubt will order this even for our mutual happiness – To whose mercy and protection, I shall not fail to recommend you by constant prayers, and intercessions for you, which are never more ardent and sincere than when you are interested in them. I shall anxiously wait for a letter from you – I hope it will be favourable – communicate your thoughts with freedom, and without the least reserve, for you may depend with unshaken confidence, upon the most inviolable secrecy from me, if required, as to anything you shall please to communicate. Should you be so disposed, I have no manner of objection to your showing this or any subsequent letter to Mr. Foulkes, in that I beg his acceptance of my Christian love and best respects; my dearest friend, pray for me, and believe me with the most sincere and invariable affection.

Your most unfeigned friend and humble servant.

Thomas Charles

28th December 1779

Wow! In eighteenth-century parlance this letter was a bit risky – writing a letter to a young lady inviting her to think about their marriage when they had only met once! For Thomas his writing to Sally was a step of faith, having set his heart on her only after hearing about her six years earlier. He kept to the rules of the time, by allowing his letters to be scrutinised by her stepfather. This was no secret affair kept from parents. Little did Thomas know that William Williams of Pant-y-celyn, the hymn writer had his eyes on her for his son John (Jack) and he hoped one day to be her proud father-in-law.

Her reply of 17 January 1780 is regrettably lost to us; to his letter of the 27 January 1780, replying, Thomas added a postscript:

> My dearest Love! I shall be wretchedly miserable till I come and see you – Days will be weeks, weeks will be months and till that blessed period arrives. However, tho' it is absolutely impossible at present, for many reasons, yet I hope, conclusion of this year I shall be able to contrive to spend 3 weeks or a month at Bala – farewell!

We can only guess what thoughts she had conveyed to Thomas's mind in her letter for him to use the words 'My dearest Love'. Thomas was smitten!

We do, fortunately, have her third letter to Thomas, who had written to her while he was unwell:

> Rev$^d$ sir,
>
> I hope your indisposition is removed, and your life prolonged for future usefulness in the land of the living – It would have afforded me more Pleasure to hear you were well, than to have a proof of your sincerity towards an unworthy object – If that Charity which hopeth all things, admits me the place of a Christian friend in your heart, it is more than I have merit to claim, and all the esteem I can desire or wish – I do not know what happiness there may be in conjugal union, whose friendship is grounded on that Christian Love you have described, I think it bids fair for happiness in the nearest connection; but it would be a bold adventure to prove it – I must look at this at some great distance, or as a thing never to come to pass, or the thought will be intolerable – The wheel of Providence is in a good Hand, and I can be easy about it – If we had it to turn for ourselves, we were undone, for we are often blind to our own happiness, and seek it where it is least to be found –Some seek it in Riches, others in honour; but these are perishing things, and always on the wing as Doctor Watts expresses it.

'Glittering stones, and golden things,
Wealth and honour that have wings
Ever fluttering to be gone
I could never call my own.'

I can't suppose these to be your aim, there are no golden mines in poor Bala – I also know what it is to despise these trifles in comparison to the beauty of Godliness, or the image of God in a believer – I detest the thought even in the darkest hour of temptation of having for a friend here, one that must be excluded from bliss to all eternity – But from whence cometh this freedom for me to write? I hope it will not be subject to the remarks of any other person besides yourself? Why is it supposed it is the outside of my letters I wish to conceal? Is not this intended to wave my request? and free you from the engagement of keeping them to yourself? I see no danger of any suspicion of our correspondence arising from thence. If I do, I'll follow your advice, without there is occasion I would rather not do it for it will rise in my Father a curiosity to see my letters – It is already as great as I can well manage – He thinks he has a right to see your letters, there is no hiding them from him – I hope your change of situation is agreeable, and that it is ordered for the good of many – I trust it is your greatest comfort in your ministry to be a blessing to Precious souls – It can't be otherwise to one who has tasted that the Lord is gracious – May the Lord plentifully water His Inheritance, and move His clouds as seemeth Him good – I dare not make an application of the last page of yr letter to myself – I know if I had faith but as a grain of mustard seed, it would enable me to do it, for Jesus is a mighty Saviour, able to keep what is given, against that Day. Nothing but unbelief doubts His willingness. 'Who seeks His face, who knows His Love, who feel on Earth His power to Love, Shall ask the Monster where is thy Sting? and where is thy Victory, boasting grave?' I am,

> Your well wisher,
> Sally Jones.

Bala, March 16, 1780.

This lovely letter shows Sally's humble yet generous and gracious spirit filled with a knowledge of God that came from a deep insight into the scriptures. She realised the importance of the course they were on, should the Lord see it through to marriage. The phrase 'there are no golden mines in poor Bala' is a gentle rebuke by Sally to Thomas should he be seeking marriage for her money; we can only wonder how he took that!

One wonders how Thomas would have felt if his approaches had been rejected and what the course his career in the Church in Great Britain might have taken. But from the moment Thomas heard about Sally we can be sure he knew that God's hand was in this relationship. From Thomas's letters we see his great love for her. It is a pity that her first two replies to his have not been preserved, so we do not know how she expressed her feelings for him, if she had any at all. We do know that her replies were always prompt and when she was away at markets selling her goods she arranged for his letters to be forwarded to her. From this we must assume his letters meant very much to her, and the Lord may have been using them to arouse her love for Thomas. Our other heroes did not have the same insoluble problem as they married local women. But God had His plan for this couple, and Thomas believed 'He [God] orders all things in the best manner for the advancement of His own glory.'

Thomas's handling of this situation is impeccable. He took into consideration that it was prudent that Mr and Mrs Foulks knew from the beginning of his intentions and that they were centred on his love and great respect for Sally. He knew because of their circumstances it must fall upon him to try to relocate to Wales. There appeared to be no resolution to this problem of separation other than for Thomas to find a parish in North Wales where he might serve the Lord. But he knew the Welsh bishops and clergy might not want him because, like others, he was seen as a Methodist and he would in due time be married to a Methodist.

For a time he made the utmost effort to find a parish in that part of Wales and to enlist the help of friends, but without success. He had the help of several friends in seeking a living, but the nearest was in South Wales, which was seen as not suitable because of the distance from Bala. He was to wait patiently nearly four years before leaving his Somerset curacy. During this time he received a letter from Sally telling him that Hannah, sister of his friend Simon Lloyd, was married and that she had the honour to be a bridesmaid. Hannah married Lewis Gwynn at Llanycil on 31 December 1782. In the same letter she tells Thomas that Simon was appointed curate to two churches in Denbighshire. Yet Thomas could not obtain a preferment in North Wales himself! Thomas busied himself preparing a commentary on the Book of Revelation with his co-authors, Thomas Reader and John Lucas.

Thomas was isolated in England. Bala was 150 miles away as the crow flies – a four-day journey by horse. He could not be away from his parish work for several weeks. These years were particularly difficult for him, having the care of country parishes, and his day-to-day routine was only brightened by visits from friends who were able to tell him of events in his homeland – Wales. Sally wrote telling him of the revival in South Wales. She calls the preachers 'flaming ministers of the Sanctuary' and says over 300 souls had been added to the Church in Llangeitho. As a Welshman he knew the feeling *hireth* – the longing for home. He knew that to some his chosen course of resigning from his curacy might be considered irresponsible, but for him it was a matter of trusting his future and Sally's to God.

It was in early 1783 that Thomas decided to give up his living in Somerset and throw himself upon God for opportunities to preach the gospel that he hoped would be given him in North Wales. This new beginning in Wales would not be without its trials and tribulations, but it was to prove the right course and his faith would be wonderfully rewarded. He may have been reminded of God's promise made in Psalm 121:7–8 – 'The Lord will keep you from harm – he will watch over your life: the Lord will watch over your coming and going both now and for evermore.' His confidence was in God.

On the morning of 23 June 1783 Thomas received a letter from Sally as he said farewell to Mr Lucas and friends in Milborne Port. He had turned down curacies in England and the southernmost parts of Wales as Sally's parents would not consent to her removal from North Wales even though she was now in her late twenties. He now abandoned England and cast himself upon the mercy and providence of God so that he could marry the woman he had wooed and won. A precious gift from God was Sally.

He did not immediately travel to Wales, and Thomas provided Sally with his itinerary. First he spent two weeks at Little Horwood, Buckinghamshire, with Mr Griffin, who had introduced him to the Reverend Newman and given advice when his relationship with his vicar became strained. Unfortunately Mr Griffin's advice was not always the best. Mr Griffin had offered him a curacy, which he declined. Thomas then travelled to Shawbury, north of Shrewsbury, Shropshire, to stay with the Reverend John Mayor, the friend who had helped him secure his student loan. In the months ahead John Mayor was to give him the opportunity to preach the gospel to his own congregation from time to time. He then visited Llangeitho to hear the ageing Daniel Rowland, then travelled south to Carmarthen to be with his family and found them well and busy with the harvest. He preached at Llanfihangel, his home parish, and met his dear Christian friend Rees Hugh, who had prayed for him through his education. He recorded the event:

> I could have almost cried for joy. It was the last interview I had with him in this world. In a month afterwards he went into Heaven.

# CHAPTER 17

# MARRIAGE AND JOBSEEKER IN NORTH WALES

*'He who finds a wife finds a good thing, And obtains favour from the Lord.'*

Proverbs 18:22

On 16 July 1783 Thomas arrived in Bala and was welcomed by Sally and her parents. Sally and Thomas were not rich by the standards of their day. Sally had been left money by her grandparents in their wills and Thomas had received £10 per annum from Mr Lucas for serving three churches; he had also saved from ex gratia gifts for his other duties the sum of £120, which was the equivalent of three or four years' stipends for a curate in England. He could not rely on his parents as they had suffered considerable financial losses. He learned that Rice Charles, his father had been taken to court by HM Customs & Excise for undeclared brewing of malt; the total sum of the fine was a huge £300 – the equivalent of ten years' income. It is possible that Thomas helped his father pay the fine. Thomas must have felt very troubled, even disappointed, by these family misdemeanours. When both parents died there was little for the administrators to administer. What might have been a rich inheritance from earlier times was gone.

The day both Sally and Thomas had so looked forward to dawned on 20 August 1783: they were married at Llanycil Church (now The Mary Jones World), Bala, in the presence of Simon and Lydia Lloyd, who had brought them together. Thomas wrote in his diary:

August 20th 1783. This morning I was married and I hope I can with truth say, 'in the Lord.' I have seen much of the Lord's goodness both in the person he has bestowed upon me and in his manner of giving her: the person most suitable in every view of all others I ever saw; and the manner in which she has been given me was best of all calculated to bring me to a right Spirit in asking her and in receiving her of my heavenly Father, every obstacle in the way was abundantly useful, and the delay though to me exceedingly tedious was exceedingly beneficial and absolutely necessary. The Lord will not suffer his people to have the little of earthly things he is pleased to bestow upon them, in the same manner the worldly people enjoy them, trials and crosses and disappointments shall be sent to drive them to the throne of grace, to bring them to deny themselves, to be resigned to his sovereign will, and to believe before they possess, in everything they shall live by faith. I do not know of any creature from whom, to my apprehension, I could expect more happiness, yet, blessed be the Lord, I hope I can say, I expect *nothing* from *her* but *everything* from the *Lord*, at least I endeavour to have a single Eye to him. A single Eye looks to the Lord *only* for everything, and has his glory principally in view in the use and enjoyment of what he receives, every grain of comfort or happiness I hope to enjoy in the married state I expect to come entirely from the Lord; and whatever crosses I shall meet with I hope to receive them also from the same gracious hand, whatever is good is a gift that comes from the Lord: if we continue to love and study each others' temporal and spiritual welfare, all is a gift which we must daily receive from him. However sincere and properly regulated our affection for each other may be one day, yet will it not continue so another if the Lord is not pleased to continue it. I am thankful the Lord hath made us both similar in some degree of this, and we have been enabled cheerfully to commit all to his hand and disposal, we expect the cross in faith and under every cross we hope for a blessing also, the while we are travelling together on earth we may be also travelling together towards heaven.

Although Thomas and Sally were now married, their letters of love would not cease. These continued for the rest of their lives. Whenever one of them was away from home they would write. On some occasions Sally's letters were sent the day Thomas went on a preaching tour. Her letters, full of her love for him, would often be there in the evening, bringing him great joy. Both were concerned for each other as their journeys over the Welsh mountains were particularly dangerous, especially when travelling alone. Often they would put their letters into the hands of mere strangers for carriage because they were so desirous that their thoughts were not lost for a day from one another. This great love story never abated. It is a great lesson to all married people, especially ministers of religion. Their love for their Lord made their love for one another even greater, not less. However, life was going to prove difficult in many respects. Even so, God was in the move to Bala and His blessing would follow.

Now that Thomas was in North Wales he secured some help from friends for service in their parishes at Llangynog (Montgomeryshire), Llandegla and Bryneglwys (Denbighshire), but these after a while were closed to him because the Church hierarchy learned he was married to a Methodist. However, he entered upon the curacy of Llanymawddwy, Merioneth, on 25 January 1784, riding over the mountains from Bala. During most of the week he stayed in the living provided, and after Wednesday Communion he would return to Bala. Although only fourteen miles from Bala by the shortest route, even in good weather it was not easy on foot or by horse. The peak of Aran Fawddwy towers over the landscape. Sally was concerned about the journey, especially in bad weather. She wrote:

> I had intended sending the horse to meet you. But as that would only be tedious to you to come over the mountain, my intention is to send it to meet you tomorrow, and to be at the foot of Bwlch by two o'clock in the afternoon.

Why send help only as far as Bwlch? Bwlch-y-groes in the eighteenth century was described as the most terrible mountain pass in North Wales. With a notorious stretch of poor track that climbs for over a mile at an average gradient of 3.7% (at its worst 20%), it is impossible for a horse. Thomas made this journey by foot in the snow on at least one journey. Today even with a modern surface the road compels all but the best cyclists to dismount until the descent to the A470 via Dinas-Mawddwy.

Journeys in winter were always dangerous, but God was in this move to Llanymawddwy. He wrote to Sally:

> I had a measure of the presence of God last Sunday in preaching. The people also appeared as if the divine truths affected them to some extent. And I understand that most of them are inclined to hear more of these things, although some gainsay. Some also threaten to deal with me in the worst manner possible; all is in the hand of the Lord. . . .

When he thought this might be a permanent position he met opposition from three influential parishioners, who managed to get his vicar to remove him after only three months' service. The main body of the congregation signed a counter-petition, but the person who was to deliver it to the vicar purposely destroyed the document that may have enabled him to continue as their curate. Their dislike for Methodists was their rationale – Thomas was married to a Methodist whose stepfather was a Methodist preacher.

His curacy at LLanymawddwy showed that Thomas was intent on staying in the Established Church however difficult the course might be. Thomas wrote for advice to his Oxford friend the Reverend Watts Wilkinson:

> I can live independently of the Church; but I am a churchman on principle, and therefore shall not on any account leave it, unless I am forced to do so.

Thomas took advice from several friends about whether he should leave the Church of England. One famous old converted former slave trader, the Reverend John Newton, suggested that it might be that the Lord wanted him elsewhere – like Yorkshire or Northumberland!

The time had come to visit Llangeitho; here he saw the Reverend Daniel Rowland, through whose preaching he had been so wonderfully brought into understanding the gospel. Now he decided to accept invitations to preach for the Methodists. It was not northern England where he was to exercise his powerful ministry, but North Wales and beyond. North Wales was still resistant to gospel preaching, and for Thomas it would not be an easy life.

With no curacy he began his ministry in a small way, as did Griffith Jones. He gathered a few Bala children to teach them from the Bible. He was very much liked by the children because of his warm smile, his soft tone of voice and his natural skill in drawing out their replies to his questions. He made up his own teaching course that was most suited to his pupils. As this group grew and the children put their faith in Jesus he taught a godly man to read and write, and then arranged for him to teach the children. As this was in Bala he was able to take a daily interest in this small school. Soon this grew to more schools and he was spending £40 per annum, mostly of his own money, on this ministry, to which trusted friends subscribed. If this work was to grow he needed regular funds – more than he could raise. Soon the number of schools was to increase to twenty and salaries increased. By this time Sally and Thomas had a family to provide for; their first son, Thomas, was baptised on 6 June 1785. Sally wrote to Thomas about their son:

> You will be glad to hear that our market is over and that I am well as when you left me only a little tired. I am in our room hearing Gwen singing for little Tommy who is sleeping sweetly . . . the Lord give us hearts to be thankful. . . .

The birth of their daughter Sarah came three weeks after the serious illness of Sally. Thomas wrote to a friend:

> She was taken extremely ill three weeks before her time: but the Lord in mercy wonderfully interposed. I was obliged to live a week (and a most trying week it was) tossed between hope and fear. She was extremely reduced and her strength was very nearly exhausted. The whole of her recovery is the Lord's doing, and I believe in answer to prayer in extremity. It is well to have an all-sufficient Friend to go to. When I gave her up to him, I received her back from him by a favourable turn being given to her illness. We cannot but see the Lord's hand in it from first to last. It was he 'killed and made alive'. She recovers but slowly, and is still very weak; but she is recovering, and what comfort she affords me.

Daughter Sarah was baptised on 17 February 1787. Although she was born severely retarded, they still delighted in her. David, their second son, was entered in the parish register on 13 October 1793 at Llanycil. By law all children (even if their parents were Methodists or Independents) had to be entered in the parish register. This was the case even if the children were not baptised. Parents paid sixpence to the incumbent, who would be fined forty shillings if he failed to keep the law.

Sally and Thomas loved their children, and when he was away Sally would write telling him of their progress:

> My Dear Dear Husband, You will think I am gone foolish to be writing every day without anything in particular to communicate to you. This is the last opportunity I expect to see and know you'll receive my foolish letters as they are written in much love and pray remember me most kindly to brother if he is with you and let him know it is no jest that little Tommy is a fine boy. One thing more about him, but you will hardly believe it, that he knows his mother. Yet it is certainly true. . . .

# CHAPTER 18

# WELSH CIRCULATING SCHOOLS RESURRECTED

*'Save now, I pray, O Lord; O Lord, I pray, send now prosperity.'*
Psalm 118:25.

In a letter to a friend Thomas explained how his schools came about:

Though Mr. Jones's [the Reverend Griffith Jones of Llanddowror] schools increased to the amazing number of two hundred and twenty before he died, yet there were many districts in this mountainous country never visited by his schools, or but once, and that for a very short time. In one of these districts [Llanymawddwy] it pleased the will of Providence to place me. Soon after I assumed the care of the parish, I attempted to instruct the rising generation, by catechising them [teaching them from the Bible about the Christian faith] every Sunday afternoon: but their not being able to read, I found to be a great obstacle to the progress of my work. This induced me to inquire into the state of the country, in this point of view. I soon found the poor people to be in general in the same state of ignorance. Two or three of the children of the wealthiest were sent to the next town to learn English, and this was all; the generality were left totally destitute of any instruction. As Mr. Jones's Schools had ceased to circulate, no relief could be obtained from that quarter. A thought occurred to my anxious mind, for so it really was, that by charitable assistance of some friends, I might be able to obtain means of employing a teacher, and to remove him from one place to another, to instruct the poor ignorant people. When I had succeeded in obtaining pecuniary aid, the great difficulty was removed by instructing a poor man myself, and employing him at first near me, that his school might be, in a manner, under my constant inspection a proper person.

Thomas and his Methodist friends learned of Robert Raike's Sunday schools in England and were interested in establishing the same in Wales. Thomas preferred his weekly schools while others preferred Sunday schools. Some thought what children learned on Sunday might be forgotten by the following Sunday. The first Sunday school was established in 1787 and they grew rapidly. This laid the biblical foundations for a great movement of the work of the Holy Spirit in Bala and the surrounding district. This occurred in other parts of North Wales, increasing the demand for Bibles – a demand which the SPCK, who had been so helpful to Griffith Jones, was unable to meet at this time. As the schools work grew, over 10,000 Bibles were needed – many more than ever before. During this time Thomas was working hard to write books, uncluding the great Bible dictionary that would be helpful to the Church. In 1885 a bronze medal bearing the image of Thomas Charles was struck to commemorate the centenary of the founding of the Sunday-school movement in Wales.

How would the money required be found other than by gifts from the Methodist Societies? A miracle was to happen five years before Thomas's death. We have first to return to the work of Griffith Jones, who set up his circulating schools. Upon his death Madam Bridget Bevan had supervised them, and on her death she had left a legacy of £10,000 to the schools. However, because this legacy was contested this bequest was held by the Court of Chancery and the schools, because of this misfortune, had gone into decline. One of the trustees, George Bowen, who was related to Thomas Charles, began proceedings to have the legacy released from the court. Progress was pitifully slow; the master of the court made a report in February 1804 and another in December 1806. A decree was made in favour of the release of the legacy for its original purpose and a scheme for the management of the charity was drawn up and embodied by order of the Lord Chancellor, dated 11 July 1807. Men of position and influence were appointed as trustees and two inspectors were appointed. The Reverend John Morgan[1] described the first of these inspectors:

> The first clerical inspector I remember was the Reverend Eleazar Evans, Vicar of Llanegwad. He was the last person I knew who wore powdered hair. The powder was silver gray, which together with his ruddy and youthful complexion, and his scrupulously clean and clerical attire, gave him a most pleasing and venerable look.

The schools were inspected every six months.

A further two years had to pass before the legacy was released. Interest had accumulated and the sum made available was an astonishing £30,000 7s. 6d. Under certain conditions this could be used for its original purpose. This outstanding Christian man, George Bowen, died two years later in his eighty-eighth year. This legacy allowed the establishment of new schools. The trustees set up a central school for training at Newport, Pembrokeshire. The foundation stone of the new schoolroom was laid by Bishop Burgess and the headmaster was John Morgan, who was in the post for forty-five years. It became a training centre for teachers until 1870. Alas, no mention on the commemorative inscription is made of Griffith Jones or Thomas Charles, although it does bear the name of Madam Bevan!

Thomas Charles, who had left the Church of England and joined the Methodists, in due time on the death of Daniel Rowland became the acknowledged leader of the Calvinistic Methodists in Wales. By the end of the nineteenth century for every Anglican church there were two Methodist chapels in Wales, plus other Nonconformist meeting places. Thomas Charles was the only ordained man among the Methodists in North Wales. Under his direction the difficult spiritual ground in the north of the country, hitherto so resistant to the preaching of Rowland and his colleagues, was ploughed, planted and watered, and it eventually produced a great harvest of souls.

It was during the summer of 1785 that Thomas preached for Daniel Rowland at the New Church in Llangeitho. The wise man, who always was a good judge of character and spirituality, is recorded as saying afterwards that 'Thomas Charles is the Lord's gift to North Wales.' Thomas wrote of his visit to Llangeitho:

> I attended the association of the Methodists at Llangeitho, Mr. Rowland's residence. There were at the association about twenty clergymen and between sixty to eighty lay-preachers, though not all that in the Connexion. You may suppose how glad I was to hear once more the old gray-headed Elijah proclaiming the deep things of God with that pathos, perspicuity, and energy peculiar to himself. I heard him twice, and three clergymen besides, also several lay-preachers, endowed with excellent gifts. . . . Preaching began on Saturday and lasted till Wednesday morning ten o'clock.

No sooner had Thomas arrived home than he was met with the sad news that Sally's mother had died.

The development of the Welsh circulating schools and the Welsh Sunday schools caused a great desire among both parents and children to read the Bible for themselves. The demand for Bibles was very great among the ordinary folk, who were so poor they could not afford the expense; and so few Bibles in Welsh were available. How was this difficulty to be resolved?

**Note:**

1. *Four Biographical Sketches* by John Morgan, Elliot Stock, London, 1892.

# CHAPTER 19

# THE TEENAGER WHOSE FAITH WAS REWARDED

*'Your word I have hidden in my heart, that I might not sin against You!'*

Psalm 119:11

Most people shared reading the Bible in groups, or some, like Mary Jones, travelled several miles each week to read a friend or relative's copy. Although the story of Mary Jones is fact, because of its fame much fiction has been added. Only the facts are reported here. Mary was the daughter of Jacob and Mary Jones, who were poor weavers who lived at Ty'n y Ddol, Llanfihangel-y-pennant, Merionethshire, a most beautiful and mountainous part of North Wales.

She was born on 16 December 1784. Five years later her father died. She was brought up as a Methodist and came to a personal faith in Christ at the age of eight. Thomas Ellis of Barmouth, one of Thomas Charles' teachers, opened a school at Abergynolwyn when Mary was about ten years old. She walked the three miles each morning, returning home in the evening after her free education. However, circulating schools by their very nature did not last more than a few months, so Mary walked the two miles to Penybryniau Manor, Bodilen Fawr, to read a Bible and memorise its verses every week. She so desired a Bible, as did her aunt, Ann Richards, that for years she put aside her earnings to buy one of her own. When she was aged sixteen (certainly no younger), and possibly after the harvest while daylight hours were still longer, she decided to set out for Bala. She had heard from a Calvinistic Methodist preacher, William Huw, that Thomas Charles had Bibles; he lived in Bala, thirty miles away over the mountains.

Let's set the scene. Llanfihangel-y-pennant, near Abergynolwyn is on the B4405, six miles inland from the seaside town of Tywyn. Today you can do the journey from the coast on the historic Talyllyn Railway, travelling through some of the most beautiful countryside in that part of Wales. The route to Bala from there today is along the A487 to Dolgellau, then on the A494 to Bala. But for Mary there were no tarmac roads and there was no public transport, and her mother was too poor to afford a horse. The most direct way was by foot over the mountains. As the crow flies it is about twenty-five miles, but for Mary, taking winding paths, it was thirty miles at least to Bala from her home. This mountainous country is on the south side of the great Cadair Idris mountain range. Even the A487 rises to nearly 300 metres. The courage and faith of this teenager is quite remarkable, but the story is true. It had to be done in one day before nightfall and when the weather was good. Most of the way she walked barefoot carrying her precious clogs (this was the custom for the poor) and her hard-earned savings. The Methodists were quite used to walking long distances as they did this to attend special gatherings of worship, often held in the open air. Arriving at Bala, she stayed with a kind-hearted old preacher, David Edward. Thomas Charles was recovering from an illness and had retired to bed early. In the morning Mr Edward took Mary to meet the famous Thomas Charles, who was now leader of the Calvinistic Methodist movement in Wales – the successor to Daniel Rowland.

The story is that Thomas Charles had only Bibles that had been reserved and were waiting to be collected. There were no other Bibles. At this news Mary broke down in tears. Her story was included in the Bible Society's bicentenary issue of *Word in Action* and on their website. Thomas Charles loved children – Sally and Thomas had children of their own. He was a tender-hearted man and he would never intentionally have caused Mary to cry. According to Thomas Charles' biographer, D. E. Jones, from his own research he concluded that Mary was able to obtain two Bibles from him. They may have been the last reserved Bibles he had as they were in very short supply. Mary had a copy for herself, and one was for her aunt, Ann Richards. The Bible she received was one of 10,000 printed for the SPCK in Oxford. In her Bible she wrote:

> I bought this in the 16th year of my age. I am the daughter of Jacob and Mary Jones his wife. The Lord gave me grace. Amen. Mary Jones His True Honour of the Bible in the year 1800 aged 16.

Mary Jones' Bible is now held for the Bible Society in the Library of Cambridge University, and her aunt's Bible is in the National Library of Wales.

Mary went on to be a great witness for her Lord in her community. It was meeting this teenager and others like her that led Thomas Charles to the work for which he would be best known. This meeting stuck in his memory. He resolved to take action that would provide a flow of Bibles to the principality, but it was to lead to more than just providing for the spiritual needs of Christians in Wales.

In the great days of revival in North Wales, Mary Jones would walk over the mountains with groups of people, through the night, stopping to gather for prayer and arriving in Bala early in the morning for great gatherings to hear the Bible taught and to worship God. She later moved to a village nearer the coast, where she kept bees and sold the honey and wax, giving a proportion of her income to missionary societies. She is known to have read through the whole Bible four times during her life. A monument to her memory was erected in 1907 on Ty'n y Ddol, the place where she lived with her parents.

Visit The Mary Jones World, Llanycil, Bala, Gwynedd, LL23 7YF – www.bydmaryjonesworld.org.uk.

# CHAPTER 20

# CITY MERCHANTS AND BANKERS TO THE RESCUE

*'Commit your works to the Lord, And your thoughts will be established.'*

Proverbs 16:3

Our story now moves to the City of London. The bankers and businessmen of the nineteenth century created wealth from the development of foreign trade, not by speculation or gambling. Manufacturers needed loans to finance trade that came from an expanding British Empire and export market. They did not receive payment for goods often until ninety, 120 or 180 days after shipment date, depending on which part of the world the goods were destined for. They needed finance to fill the gap until the buyer's payment was received. The finance was provided by drawing bills of exchange that were discounted by bankers. Among these were two men who took their faith very seriously – Joseph Hardcastle and Joseph Reyner. They served on missionary and welfare societies, where their faith and wealth were put into action. Seventy-five years after Mary Jones met Thomas Charles the heads of the banks in the City set up a society to promote the gospel among their own staff, and in some banks prayer preceded work.[1]

In 1789 Selina, the Countess of Huntingdon, invited Thomas Charles to preach at her Spa Fields Chapel in London for eight weeks, but at this time he declined as he was not in good health. Sally had to write to the Countess of Huntingdon explaining

Thomas's indisposition. Spa Fields Chapel, Finsbury, London, was one of sixty independent chapels founded by the Countess. Thomas did eventually preach there, and each year spent a month preaching to the congregation.

One of the members of this chapel was Joseph Tarn, who was director of the Missionary Society (later renamed the London Missionary Society) and whose daughter was to be a missionary in Malacca, Malaya. Her daughter Maria Jane Dyer married James Hudson Taylor, the founder of the China Inland Mission. Joseph was also a member of the Religious Tract Society, which was formed on 9 May 1799. The influence in forming this society was Hannah More, a Bristol playwright and a friend of the actor David Garrick. Her tracts spoke about the evils of her day – slavery and the exploitation of the poor. After her conversion to Christianity she put her energies into educating the poor and distributing the scriptures. She often came to the author's home town, Farnborough. Farnborough Place (now St Peter's School, Farnborough, Hampshire) was the home of the Wilmot family, and she met members of society there with the aim of making her faith known. There was also formed one year later the Evangelical Tracts Gratis Society. It was Joseph Tarn who skilfully brought these two organisations together. Thomas Charles was a member since their amalgamation, and he and Joseph Tarn became good friends. The committee of this society met regularly at Ducksfoot Lane (a corruption of Duke's Foot), just off the south side of Cannon Street. These meetings were held by candlelight before breakfast at 7 a.m. They liked an early start in those days! Later these meetings took place at Mr Hardcastle's Counting House (another name for a mercantile financial institution) by Old Swan Stairs at London Bridge. Yorkshireman Joseph Hardcastle was a founding member of the London Missionary Society and had business connections with many countries. It was this society that sent John Morrison to China and supported him. Hardcastle was in partnership with another Christian, Joseph Reyner, an importer of cotton. Mr Shrubsole of the Bank of England described these two merchants as 'lovers of Jesus'. Hardcastle and Reyner were school friends, educated in Leeds. Reyner had recently moved their business from 11 Philpot Lane to their address at Old Swan Stairs. Joseph Reyner was a trustee and deacon of the Independent Kingsland Chapel. While he did not have the gift of preaching, he was a good personal worker, presenting the gospel to men and leaving them a gospel tract to read clearly showing the sacrifice that Jesus had made for their sins. He was a good judge of character and was able to point many men to the way they should follow in their professional lives.

Joseph Hardcastle was a Methodist and lived at Hatcham House, New Cross, which he leased from the Haberdashers Company. Both men worked hard for the abolition of slavery.

On 9 November 1802, Thomas Charles had it in his mind to bring up the matter of the shortage of Bibles in Wales at the committee, but for some reason he did not do so. Looking at the situation that reigned in the new society at that time, this would not have been the best action. Two weeks later Joseph Tarn, who was greatly respected by all the committee, in the absence of Thomas Charles brought up the matter. The outcome was that Thomas Charles was invited to speak on Tuesday 14 December at an extraordinary meeting of the society. However, it was not until the meeting on 28 December that it was decided to consider establishing a separate society. The minutes read:

> To promote the circulation of the Holy Scriptures in foreign countries and in those parts of the British Dominions, for which adequate provision is made, it being understood that no English translation of the Scriptures will be gratuitously circulated by the Society in Great Britain.

Thomas Charles was at this meeting as he had stayed over from the previous Sunday when he had preached at Spa Fields Chapel.

It was not the intention of the Religious Tract Society to take on the work of translating, printing and distributing the scriptures. The committee considered that the work of the society was to bring the matter to the notice of Christian leaders. Joseph Reyner out of his own pocket paid the cost of 1,000 letters that were sent to prominent Christians, including Lord Wilberforce, who attended a meeting on 21 April 1803. He helped draw up the prospectus for the Bible Society in that year and was elected a vice-president of the society. Some uncertainties about future plans were delayed because of the outbreak of war with Napoleon in May 1803. The first meeting of the new society was held at The London Tavern, Bishopsgate, City of London, on 7 March 1804. In the chair was Mr Granville Sharp and Lord Wilberforce was present. The meeting continued from midday until 2 p.m. The society was to be known as the British and Foreign Bible Society. Joseph Tarn immediately wrote to Thomas Charles, who was in Bala:

> We cannot, my dear Brother, but rejoice together, when we consider that this work had its beginning in a conversation which took place between us two, one week-day morning that is ever to be remembered. Hence I was induced in the next Meeting of the members of the Tract Society to mention the scarcity of Welsh Bibles; and then was kindled that flame which has now burst forth, and which, I trust, will burn brighter and brighter until that brightest day of universal knowledge, when we shall no longer teach our brother, saying, 'Know the Lord, for all shall know him, from the least to the greatest of them.' To the Lord be all the glory: as for us, who are unworthy of the least of his mercies, it is our duty to count it a priceless privilege to be, in the slightest degree, instrumental in spreading the knowledge of the salvation of which, we trust, we are partakers.
>
> Henceforth let us join in supplicating that the stone which is, as it were, 'cut out of the mountain, without hands,' and which we saw to-day become a hill, may grow until it becomes a mountain, to cast down the strongholds of sin and Satan, from east to west, and from pole to pole; and so, though we shall not live to see that glorious day, we shall rejoice together because we were permitted to put the first stone in a structure which will continue, we hope, and be a joy to the whole earth. Begging your prayers and those of the Welsh brethren for the success of the work.

How prophetic were Joseph Tarn's words, 'from east to west, and from pole to pole'! We can see this has been realised today as Bibles are translated, printed and distributed all over the globe.

Bible societies are established all over the world. However, the work is not yet complete as there are almost 2,000 tongues that do not have a complete Bible. Thomas Charles replied:

> I cannot express the joy I felt on receiving the information of a Society being formed for supplying various nations of the world with Bibles. I hope it will prove a lasting magazine of Welsh Bibles, and relieve my anxiety on that head. Those noble institutions, the Missionary, the Sunday-School, together with the Bible Society, added now to the other two, complete the means for the dispersion of divine knowledge far and near. The Sunday-Schools have occasioned more calls for Bibles within these five years, than perhaps ever was known before, among our poor people. The possession of a Bible produces a feeling among them, which the possession of no one thing in the world besides could produce. In many houses they have but one Bible for the use of a numerous family; of course, every one cannot obtain the free use of it at all vacant seasons, when they might read it; and, frequently, the young people and the menial servants, who are debarred the use of it, are the most anxiously desirous for the reading of it. The last Oxford edition was bought up, by them principally, in every parish where dispersed, with the greatest avidity; and there were not half enough to answer the demands for them. I have seen some of them overcome with joy, and burst into tears of thankfulness, on their obtaining possession of a Bible as their own property and for their free use. Young females, in service, have walked over thirty miles to me with only the bare hope of obtaining a Bible each; and returned with more joy and thanksgiving than if they had obtained great spoils. We, who have half a dozen Bibles by us, and are in circumstances to obtain as many more, know but little of the value those put upon one, who before were hardly permitted to look into a Bible once a week.

Notice that Thomas Charles had already shortened the name of the society to the Bible Society. Joseph Hardcastle was so overjoyed with the establishment of the new society that on 13 March 1804 he wrote to his eldest daughter:

> I have the pleasure to inform you of the formation of a new institution, the object of which is to promote the more general circulation of the Scriptures in Great Britain and foreign countries. It has for some time been the subject of attention in the

committee of the Tract Society and by means of a circular letter a numerous meeting was held on Wednesday at the London Tavern which was remarkably harmonious and impressive – a committee of 36 persons was formed consisting of individuals connected with almost every religious denomination and about £700 were immediately subscribed.

This institution seems likely to meet with extensive support and to be the occasion of bringing close connection these good men of different parties who have been too long disassociated. This may be considered as another stream which has flowed from the missionary fountain, as it is entirely owing to the committee of the Tract Society.

Your affectionate Father,
Joseph Hardcastle

Joseph Reyner was appointed a member of the committee and Joseph Tarn was made an assistant secretary of the new society for the publication of the scriptures. On Wednesday 1 May 1805 the first annual meeting of the society met at the New London Tavern and the first annual report was delivered by Lord Teignmouth, the president. He was able to give this good news:

Your committee, therefore, on being apprised that the University of Cambridge had entered into an agreement with Mr. Wilson, the stereotype printer, resolved . . . [that] twenty thousand Welsh Bibles of a smaller size than octavo would be printed for the Society at the University Press . . . [furthermore] very liberal contributions made in Wales amounting to nineteen hundred pounds; and the more so, as it has been made with great zeal and cheerfulness, which manifest the sincerest veneration for the Holy Scriptures, and more than a common anxiety to possess them. The amount of the contributions is more remarkable when we advert to the poverty of the majority of the subscribers.

So the first act of the new society was to provide 20,000 Bibles and then 5,000 New Testaments (later increased to 10,000) in Welsh. Christians in Wales were going to wait a few more years for a plentiful supply of Bibles in their own language as various matters had to be decided upon, such as which edition of the Welsh Bible was to be published and there would be corrections to the text. And then the printing process had to be decided upon. The printing subcommittee met on 11 December 1805 at Hardcastle and Reyners, Old Swan Stairs in the City. After receiving a letter from the Bishop of St David's, they decided that the 1752 edition was to be used. The Society for Promoting Christian Knowledge had also decided to print a new edition; therefore certain matters had to be resolved between the two societies. Although the Bible Society put the printing into the hands of the Cambridge University Press and they were to receive plates from Andrew Wilson, the stereotypist, there was a further delay as Mr Wilson disputed the ownership of the plates and would not part with them. The society appointed the Reverend W. F. Platt and Mr Anthony Wagner to resolve the dispute. It took until the following July to resolve the matter. Although the New Testaments show May 1806 as the publication date, it was not until September that the first of the New Testaments were being dispatched from the printer's warehouse. Orders were being dispatched to shops, clergy and private people all over Wales. Usually an order was for at least 100 Bibles, and in some cases for hundreds. The society and printers were finding it difficult to keep up with the demand.

**Note:**

1. The records of the London Banks' Prayer Union are held in the Metropolitan Archives, London.

# CHAPTER 21

# AN INSATIABLE DEMAND FOR BIBLES

*'And now, Lord, what do I wait for? My hope is in You.'*
Psalm 39:7.

Why was the demand for Bibles so great in Wales? There are several reasons. The rise in the literacy rate had increased due to the re-establishment of circulating schools and the foundation of the Sunday-school movement. There is another reason – that was God was renewing the Church in Wales. Reading through the correspondence of Thomas Charles with friends throughout Wales there is no doubt that the growth of the Church in Wales was not slackening. According to historians the period 1785–1815 was the most fruitful in the Welsh Church. In 1791 Thomas Charles wrote a short account of a powerful spiritual awakening in Bala:

> Towards the close of the evening service the Spirit of God seemed to work in a very powerful way on the minds of great numbers present, who never appeared before to seek the Lord's face.

In 1812 there were powerful movements of the Holy Spirit, and it is worth quoting a letter, dated March, written by Thomas Charles to London friends after a preaching tour:

> The prospect in South Wales, in a religious point of view, is most delightful. In some parts was truly presented to us a faithful representation of the day of Pentecost; there was a rushing wind that bore down all before it. Into one Society, above 140 were received in the space of about two months. All the young

people in a large district were under religious impressions. The Association at Aberystwyth and Haverfordwest were very pleasing and profitable. The congregation at the former, amounted to about 20,000 persons; and great order and solemnity prevailed during the whole of the meetings. I have seen something similar in former days; but nothing like it for years past. Preaching was as easy as opening the lips, and divine influences on preachers and hearers, were felt mightily. Without being in the work, and partakers of the influences, no one can form any conception of it. For my own part, whilst I have any memory, I shall never forget it! It is the more delightful to me, as I view it, in a great measure, as the happy fruit of our Sunday Schools. I pray the Lord it may spread wider and wider, till it covers the land! More has been done in a few weeks since the work began, than was done before in many years of painful labour, although perhaps it is the produce of those years of faithful labour. The Lord hath done great things for us, whereof we are glad! Our mouths are filled with laughter! Excuse my warmth in writing on the subject,– when I think of it my whole soul is kindled in a flame.

Thomas Charles wrote to a minister in Scotland:

That it is the work of God I am not left in doubt in the least degree: it carries along with it every scriptural satisfactory evidence that we can possibly desire; such as deep conviction of sin, of righteousness and of judgment; great reformation of manners [behaviour]; great love for, and delight in the love of God, in prayer, in spiritual conversion and divine ordinances.

Much could be written about the lives of Thomas and Sally Charles: their daughter died a year after being born, and both Thomas and Sally in later life suffered from ill health possibly due to their energetic labours for their Saviour. Sally was unwell for three years and Thomas looked after her although he too was not in full health. He passed to be with the Lord on Wednesday 5 October 1814; just over two weeks later Sally followed him into the presence of the Lord.

Before the burial at the parish church a vast number of people assembled to pay their last respects at a devotional service conducted by the Reverend John Roberts of Llangwm, and a sermon was preached by the Reverend Thomas Jones of Denbigh on Hebrews 11:4: 'By faith He still speaks, even though He is dead.' Speaking about his departed friend's faith, Thomas Jones said:

> Wales has cause to weep for him for this loss; and a loss it is. If Wales ever had cause to weep it is now. He prayed much for his family, for the town of Bala, God bless the town he said grieved [over the spiritual state]: his prayers will be answered too, either through blessings on the town, or by visitation in judgment. This man's loss will be a loss to Britain, to many notable men in London; the memory of him will be green for ages. God can make the fruits of his prayers appear more abundant than he ever saw them in his day. I must add that God so honoured his servant during his last days as enabled him to leave behind him a strong testimony of his hope of eternal life. Among his last words were those of Simeon of old – repeated more than once two days before he died, 'Lord, now lettest thou thy servant depart in peace, according to thy word: for mine eyes have seen thy salvation.' I remember hearing some people, who heard his last sermon thirty miles from here, on those words in Romans 8:18, 'For I reckon, that the sufferings of this present time are not worthy to be compared with the glory which shall be revealed to us': saying that he was most heavenly in his remarks on those words, and that he seemed like one ripe and ready to escape from the bodily sufferings which then harassed him, to enjoy the glory that shall be revealed to all the people of God.

As the solemn procession formed for the journey to Llanycil Church there was not a dry eye in the whole concourse. Appropriate hymns were sung all the way to the Church – a distance of about a mile – and so great was the crowd that only a small proportion of it could gain admittance; the rest remained outside until the service within was over. During that service an anthem taken from Psalm 39 was sung; the ceremony at the grave ended with another hymn. He will be forever known as Thomas Charles of Bala.

# CHAPTER 22

# THE GREAT LEGACY

*'Oh, give thanks to the Lord! Call upon His name; Make known His deeds among the peoples! Sing to Him, sing psalms to Him; Talk of all His wondrous works! Glory in His holy name; Let the hearts of those rejoice who seek the Lord!'*

Psalm 105:1–3

Thomas Charles had lived long enough to witness the ordination of the first Methodist ministers. The subject of ordination of exhorters (as Methodist preachers were called) was brought before the Association held at Swansea in 1810, at which Thomas was asked to give his opinion; this was provoked by a question from Ebenezer Morris, who asked in a solemn and commanding voice, "Which is the greatest and most important work? Is it the preaching of the gospel or administering the ordinances of baptism and the Lord's Supper?"

After some thought Thomas Charles rose from his seat and answered, "The greatest work is preaching the gospel."

Ebenezer Morris's reply was "*We are one.* Satan had thought to divide us, but thanks be unto God, *we are one.*"

The brethren felt a sense of unity, and this matter, which had been discussed much over the years, was not to divide them now. Their decision was unanimous: ordain. Those who had been ordained in the episcopal Church would ordain Methodist preachers.

The following year eight preachers from North Wales were ordained; among them was John Elias, who had regretted not having heard Daniel Rowland preach because at the time he was too young to travel the long distance from Caernarvonshire. John Elias was described by many as a 'messenger from God'. David Charles said of him, 'In all my journeys through Wales I have never heard of any other preacher whose ministry has been so widely blessed to the conversion of sinners as that of John Elias.' Thirteen were chosen from South Wales, including Thomas's brother David Charles, who was greatly used by God in preaching the gospel. By 1850 the Welsh Calvinistic Methodist Connection had 172 ordained ministers, 194 preachers, 848 chapels and places set aside for preaching and a membership (communicants) of 58,678. Daniel Rowland's son Nathaniel was against their ordination, but the break was the inevitable consequence of the Established Church rejecting for ordination those they considered were Methodists.

The Bible Society that Thomas Charles and Joseph Tarn brought about grew rapidly. The first twenty-three years of its activities in the UK provide some amazing figures:

> Supporting branches, 3,965.
> Bibles provided, 2,095,745.
> New Testaments provided, 3,144,383.
> Funds spent on scriptures, £1,424,985 4s. 7d.

On 27 April 1810 the first auxiliary in Wales of the Bible Society was established in Swansea. Within a few years Bibles Societies were being established in Scotland, Russia, the Netherlands and the United States of America, and this continued to expand into other countries across the globe. Countries were beginning to receive Bibles freely that their people could read in their own languages, thanks to these godly men who knew the leading of the Holy Spirit. May God raise up men like Tarn and Charles in our day. The whole thrust of missionary activity was greatly increased by giving God's servants the greatest tool any missionary could have – the Word of God in the languages of the people to whom they had been sent to preach the gospel. Missionaries now had available a source for the publication of Bibles in the languages they themselves had put into writing. This would help to establish new Christians in their faith and build the Church in distant lands.

In 1844 – only forty years after the establishment of the Bible Society – Pope Gregory XVI issued his encyclical *Inter Praecipuas* warning the Roman Catholic Church of the danger posed by the translations produced by the 'biblical societies', as he called them. Bill Cooper writes:

> One thing that alarmed the Vatican at that time more than anything else on earth, was the sudden burgeoning of the Bible Societies, both in Britain and the U.S.A. These existed solely for the purpose of disseminating the Word of God in every language possible, and their immediate effect was to destablise the many nations of the world over which the Church of Rome held sway. Their funds seemed inexhaustible, and their work was immensely enhanced by the great wave of evangelical and missionary fervour which was gripping the west.[1]

The chain started by Griffith Jones, with the links of Daniel Rowland and Thomas Charles was continued through the establishment of the Bible Society, which distributed the living Word of God throughout the world. A huge multitude of worshippers will fall at the feet of Jesus because of this chain.

Praise, glory and honour to God alone.

**Note:**

1. *The Forging of Codex Sinaiticus* by Bill Cooper, Creation Science Movement, Portsmouth, 2016.

# CHAPTER 23

# THE CHALLENGE

*'On the last day, that great day of the feast, Jesus stood and cried out, saying. "If anyone thirsts, let him come to Me and drink. He who believes in Me, as the Scripture has said, out of his heart will flow rivers of living water." But this He spoke concerning the Spirit, whom those believing in Him would receive.'*

John 7:37–39

Anyone with a good knowledge of the Church in Wales in the eighteenth century will know that not everything was perfect and went well. Some well-meaning Christians argued over particular aspects of theology, eventually breaking fellowship with one another; others went off to do their own work when being part of a team may have been best; and some even disgraced themselves by their lifestyle and called into question whether they had stopped 'looking unto Jesus, the Author and Finisher of their faith'. Not even our three heroes were blameless, because we all fail God and one another from time to time.

However, the lives of our three men were greatly blessed in their ministry, resulting in widespread blessing in Wales and beyond. They were faithful like the Old Testament prophets. I believe there are lessons we can learn from the content of their sermons and their diaries, and what we know from the biographical record of their lives. It is clear to any student studying this period of Welsh Church history that God honoured these men and blessed their ministry with dynamic power. Our heart's cry should be that we see God working with that same power in our own churches today. I have read their sermons and found nothing exceptional compared with those of other evangelicals of their time. It was that God honoured their theology, their preaching, and this brought blessing. They lived close to God and were holy men that He could honour.

They not only spoke with great love and compassion to their congregations on the grace and love of God, but they were not afraid to preach God's judgement on sinners, the need for repentance and the awfulness of rejecting His forgiveness. People trembled at their preaching! The call to repent was part and parcel of Griffith Jones' preaching. He wrote:

> Repentance has been preached under every dispensation: It was preached by the prophets: it was preached by John the Baptist: it was preached by Christ himself: it was preached by his apostles: it has been preached in all ages: it ought to be preached still, and even until the end of the world.

Again in his sermon Griffith Jones reminded us powerfully from scripture that repentance was preached by the prophets, the Apostles and Our Lord:

> Ezekiel was given the commission by God to preach to Israel a message of repentance, 'Therefore say to the house of Israel, this is what the Sovereign Lord says: Repent! Turn from your idols and renounce all your detestable practices!'

John the Baptist, a prophetic preacher under the Old Testament dispensation warned his hearers, "Produce fruit in keeping with your repentance" (Matthew 3:8).

Jesus preached the need for repentance: "I tell you that in the same way there will be more rejoicing in heaven over one sinner who repents than over ninety-nine righteous persons who do not need to repent" (Luke 15:7).

The Apostles preached repentance: Peter cried, "Repent and be baptised, every one of you, in the name of Jesus Christ for the forgiveness of sins. And you will receive the gift of the Holy Spirit" (Acts 2:38).

Paul, referring to his ministry, wrote, "I have declared to both Jews and Greeks that they must turn to God in repentance and have faith in our Lord Jesus" (Acts 20:21).

Our heroes, like the Reverend George Whitefield (1714–70), believed in the fall of man. He visited Wales to meet his friends with whom he shared the same theology, and took a keen interest in the revival that was sweeping Wales. Preaching on Genesis 3: 15, he said:

> The fall of man is written in too legible [bold] characters . . . those that deny it, by their denying prove it. The very heathens confessed and bewailed it; they could see the streams of corruption running through the whole race of mankind, but could not trace them to the fountain-head. Before God gave a revelation of his Son, man was a riddle to himself. And Moses unfolds more, in one chapter (out of which this text is taken) than all mankind could have been capable of finding out for themselves, though they had studied to all eternity. In the preceding chapter [Genesis chapter 2] he had given us a full account how God spoke the world into being; and especially how he formed man of the dust of the earth, and breathed into him the breath of life, so that he became a living soul. A council of the Trinity was called concerning the formation of this lovely creature. The result of that council was, 'Let us make man in our image, after our likeness. So God created man in his own image, in the image of God created he him.' Moses remarkably repeats these words, that we might take particular notice of our divine Original. Never was so much expressed in so few words.

Daniel Rowland spoke against a gospel that required 'only an intellectual assent' to be sufficient for salvation; an eighteenth century 'easy-believism'. This was an unbalanced view of the gospel according to Daniel Rowland. Jones, Rowland, and Charles preached that true repentance before a holy God was necessary, and that the sinner had not only to understand with his mind but also to open his heart and *will* to the good news of Jesus Christ. The precursor to this was repentance. Our three heroes stood firm on the Thirty-nine Articles of Religion (the declaration of faith of the Anglican Church). They believed in original sin and that men and women need to confess they are sinners, deserving the righteous judgement of God. They believed we had inherited the fallen nature of Adam. They believed in God's righteous condemnation and judgement of unrepentant sinners. Under their preaching people knew the deep conviction of sin that came from hearing the gospel. This conviction, the acceptance of their fallen state and their desire to repent were the work of the Holy Spirit. They did not need to make gospel appeals, because before the time the sermon was over people were crying out in repentance, asking for forgiveness from God and coming into a glorious assurance of faith.

Is there that conviction, that contrition today that is the result of preaching the gospel of Jesus Christ? Do we see it in the Church? Have repentance and judgement slipped gradually from the teaching of the Church? Is there too much emphasis today on the love of God? These are questions that we need to seriously consider. Many Christians are not wholly convinced that the entire Bible is the authoritative Word of God any longer and prefer to drop those difficult chapters that seem to be out of character with a loving God. Our heroes if they visited us today would be appalled and ashamed at what they heard being taught and the resulting loss of dynamic power in our preaching. They would see the lack of passion and urgency in the preaching compared with their time, and they would be disappointed that Jesus Christ is not the Sum and Substance of sermons.

The gospel of our Lord Jesus Christ was so precious to them that they could only proclaim it with passion, energy and clarity; to do otherwise was inconceivable. The message they had received by grace that resulted in their lives being turned over to the Lord Jesus Christ was passed on to others by what was probably some of the most powerful and dynamic preaching experienced since Pentecost. Every word preached was an arrow aimed at the hearts and minds of their hearers. They spoke with one voice, with one message, with one aim – to glorify God. Nobody could be in any doubt as to the urgency of their message. They proclaimed the Lord Jesus Christ, His death and Resurrection. Only He has the power to forgive sins and He is the only Way to salvation. Wherever they preached and whenever they preached,

Jesus Christ was the subject matter. The power of the Holy Spirit confirmed their message by bringing thousands to the foot of the Cross in repentance and faith. They were not only evangelists, but teachers in the apostolic tradition, grounding converts in the faith by encouraging them to join Societies where they received biblical teaching and grew in the grace of the Lord Jesus Christ to become mature men and women fit to proclaim the message themselves.

It is notable that the revival brought a heightening of awareness of the place of Holy Communion in the life of the Church. No one can read about the revivals that took place in Wales from the mid-eighteenth century onwards without noticing how central the Holy Communion service became in the life of the renewed Church. All three men held monthly Communion services that were wonderfully blessed. Thomas Charles made sure he was home in Bala to celebrate Holy Communion on the first Sunday of each month. Even though he had left the Church of England, he still used the form of service and prayers laid down in the Book of Common Prayer. It was when the Lord's suffering, death and Resurrection were being celebrated that the manifestations of the Holy Spirit were often experienced with tears, later leading to great joy. The celebrant and congregation were often overcome with a great feeling of unworthiness and conviction of sin. Not until confession was made and people were in the right relationship with God did they experience blessing, joy and peace and this was expressed in a pouring-out of thankful praise. Yes, they were often accused of 'jumping' for joy, but their leaders accepted that this was the inevitable response to knowing your sins were forgiven and God had clothed the repentant sinner with His cloak of righteousness.

There is pain in the spiritual realm; there is pain in regeneration, as there is in physical birth. When Griffith Jones penned these words no doubt he had the Holy Communion in his mind:

> To catch all opportunities of doing good to others, to watch carefully against the strugglings of our hearts from God, and to make a very solemn use of consecrated ordinances, are methods

that will hardly fail to bring us on towards the attainment of joyful hope and full assurance of faith, which is the life of a religious profession ... there cannot be greater happiness or greater honour than to be chosen by the ever-glorious King of Heaven to carry on the advancement and promotion of His Kingdom on earth, and do all that is practicable to bring forth the miserable captives of dismal darkness into marvellous healing light, that they may enjoy the inconceivable benefits of His death and passion.

When we take the bread and wine there should be a deep reverence and love for God and for one another. We remember that Christ shed His blood for us, and His body was broken for us. We are reminded to repent of our sins at the foot of the Cross as we seek His forgiveness for the wrong we have done since we last met. We acknowledge it is the work of the Holy Spirit to do His work in us, to fashion us into the likeness of our Saviour. In the last few years I have found the observance of the sacrament of Holy Communion very moving. I remember once at the close of worship instead of people departing for fellowship over beverages and biscuits, twos and threes stayed together praying with each other.

Don't let anything detract from the careful observance of the celebration that Jesus commanded us to keep. Let us not eat and drink unworthily – *let us take time*. God may have commanded the Israelites under the leadership of Moses to eat the Passover in haste and dressed ready for their journey. We have no journey like them to make from an oppressive regime that enslaves us – we have been liberated from spiritual captivity!

The words that rang in the ears of the unconverted Howell Harris that so stirred him from lethargy were from his vicar, Pryce Davies: "If you are not fit to come to the Lord's Table, you are not fit to come to church; you are not fit to live, nor fit to die." Pryce Jones knew the great worth of this sacrament to his congregation.

Moving nearer to this century, the Reverend Dr Ernest Kevan preaching at Coonoor, India, to pastors of the Grace Baptist Mission, placed emphasis on why this sacrament is so special. He called it 'a strengthening remembrance':

It cannot but be that the doing of this thing was intended by the Lord to be a means of grace to us. And though it is true that the elements are no more than the signs of our redemption, the ordinance itself is not a *bare* commemoration. I am placing emphasis upon the adjective 'bare'. I am convinced that what is often called the Zwinglian view of the Lord's Supper, that is, the commemorative view of the significance of the elements, is perfectly correct. But we rise above the elements. The service is not complete merely in bread and wine. The active faith of the believer in taking the elements is of immense significance. He is feeding upon the Lord Jesus Christ himself. Thus, while the elements are mere representations, the service is more than representation. It was Mr. Spurgeon (if I may hide behind him for orthodoxy here) who urged his people in one of his sermons on the Lord's Supper to 'feast on Him', and it is this spiritual reality which is expressed in the familiar Anglican formula, 'feed on Him in your hearts by faith'. Again to quote from Mr. Spurgeon's well-known sermon, 'We not only eat of His bread, but symbolically, we feast upon Him. . . . I believe in the real presence of Christ: I do not believe in the carnal presence of the Romanist. I believe in the real presence to the believer: but that reality is none the less real because it is spiritual.' How blessed a thing it has been for you to gather again and again around the Lord's Table with the Lord's people! Has not it been a means of grace to you? Has not it been a channel through which the Lord has shown you His glory and renewed your faith and sweetened your love? Of course it has.[1]

Speaking at the Grace Baptist Assembly in 2011, the Reverend Stuart Olyott impressed upon his hearers the importance of the Lord's Supper:

> His body broken in my stead,
> Is seen in this memorial bread,
> And so, our feeble love is fed,
> Until He come!
>
> His drops of dread agony,
> His life-blood shed for us we see;
> The wine shall tell the mystery,
> Until He come!
>
> *George Rawson, 1857.*

Jesus Christ must always be central in His Church, and we are called to stop everything – *everything!* Every Christian is called to stop everything, to have a meal together where we do nothing at all except remember him in the way He appointed. The candlestick [Revelation 2:5] disappeared, you know, if there is no love for Christ. In this wonderful way we are given to remind us who we are, and who He is, what we've done, what He's done, so simple, so profound, so soul-shaking, so exercising, not individual, yet very individual, corporate. It took a Genius to invent the Lord's Supper.

There was another matter that these men considered essential, and that was that each person should have their faith embedded in the Word of God; they wanted their people to memorise verses from the Bible, to digest them, to understand them, to live by them and to read the Bible daily in their families. The reason Societies were organised was to ensure each person was progressing in their walk with God. The leaders were looking for lives that exhibited the fruit of the Holy Spirit in these new believers. These Societies were very personal, but often people were counselled and confession was made in the group. How embarrassing many would find this in their home groups today! The leaders of these Societies, called exhorters, were chosen because they could give a clear testimony of their conversion and they had the gifts and biblical knowledge that enabled them to lead others into a deeper life in Christ. Many of these men who bore pastoral oversight later became ordained ministers. Are our home-group leaders trained in the spiritual skills needed to nurture those young in the faith and do they have a very real knowledge of the Bible? Are they able to answer the tough questions put by those young Christians who have been saved from an atheistic culture?

People were so keen to learn from the Bible that it seemed impossible to meet the demand for copies. This is true of so many places today, like Iran, China and Africa. But today, thanks to God working through the obedient Joseph Tarn and Thomas Charles of Bala, most of the demand for Bibles can be satisfied. People can also have the Bible in their own language, if it has been translated in its entirety. How important translation work and the

Bible Societies are today! Are we concerned that every Christian should experience the delights of reading the Bible every day in their mother tongue and that they are feeding on God's very words wherever they might be on the earth? Are our churches making reading and understanding of the content of the Bible a priority? Is every member feeding on God's Word daily?

The late Reverend Selwyn Hughes, Life President of the Crusade for World Revival (CWR), speaking at the bicentenary of the British and Foreign Bible Society, at Guildford Cathedral, described the Bible as "a book we will never finish with, as God continually speaks to us through the Bible. The Bible read daily tones our lives; it is God's dynamic word for our lives."

Every Christian should learn to digest the Bible daily, learn to memorise it and hide it in their hearts, chewing it over as a cow chews the cud, getting the nourishment that the life in Christ demands.

We cannot overestimate the powerful effect that teaching had on the lives of children and adults in circulating schools and Sunday schools. Today there are over 4,600 Church of England schools in the UK, as well as schools of other Christian denominations. If only the pupils in these schools caught the gospel message as they did in the circulating schools, what a difference it would make to our nation! We should pray for governors, heads and staff and groups that go into schools to take assemblies – the place where most pupils will first hear a Bible story.

Today our prayers should also be focused on our education system, which is under pressure from atheistic groups. Schools and churches with their teachers and youth ministers are not alone responsible for teaching our children the Christian faith. *As parents we have to accept our responsibility for teaching our children the Christian faith as delivered by Christ and His Apostles.* It was family worship that particularly warmed the hearts of our three heroes. We should not leave teaching our children to the Church alone.

These men all had an experience of the risen Christ in their lives. This was an experience that came from their realising they were sinners – they knew they had inherited Father Adam's fallen nature. They knew that the antidote to this was Christ's power to change them, and this He did dramatically. God's love was unconditional and their response was unconditional surrender of their whole being to Him. Their surrender to the risen Christ was such that they emptied themselves of *self* and they became disciples filled with the Holy Spirit; to be other than that, they knew, was to deny themselves the blessing of God on their ministries. No wonder they were often under extreme attack from the adversaries of Christ. They were marked men. They would not compromise on any matter that was contrary to the Word of God or that would deny the power attributable to Him. They never allowed compromise that would spoil their relationship with their Saviour, the Lord Jesus Christ. How often have we heard someone say of a Christian, "They are fully committed"? I don't like the phrase because it conveys the idea that we 'have arrived'. If we knew our own hearts we would know that God can put His finger on so many things that He needs us to put right or surrender to His control.

Our heroes had opened up their lives to the searching gaze of the Holy Spirit; He had put His finger on everything that would hinder their intimate relationship with the Lord Jesus Christ. So many today are unaware that the Holy Spirit needs to do a refining process in their lives, producing the fruit that is glorifying to God. As we get older in years we are often aware of how much work the Holy Spirit needs to do and how far we have come. I remember the Reverend Duncan Campbell speaking in London on the matter of holiness, taking as his text the contest between the prophets of Baal and Elijah on Mount Carmel (1 Kings 18). When speaking on holiness he referred to this event again when speaking at the Keswick-in-Wales convention in 1956, from which I quote:

> Someone has said that at Pentecost God set the Church at Jerusalem on fire and the whole city came out to see it burn. I tell you if that happened in any church today, within hours the whole of the town would be out to see the burning, and they would be caught in the flames. It is fire we want. The best advertising campaign that any church or any mission can put up is fire in the pulpit and a blaze in the pew. Let us be honest. We say God send revival, but are

we prepared for the fire? Think for a moment of that which took place at Carmel, that mighty manifestation of God. When did the fire fall? When the altar was built? No! When the bullock lay dead beneath the altar? No!

I see the man of God take his knife and he cuts the bullock in pieces; did the fire fall? No! The pieces are placed on the altar, piece one, piece two, piece three, but the heavens are as brass, the fire has not fallen. The process goes on. There is another piece here; I see the Prophet handle it and it is placed on the altar, but the fire has not fallen. Right there, just at the back of the altar, there is another small piece. I see the prophet move round and I see him handling that piece. It is the last piece, and now the last piece is placed upon the altar. The miracle happens. The heavens are rent and God comes down, the fire falls, and there is a mighty manifestation followed by a mighty revival.

Will you honestly and sincerely face this question? You are interested in revival, you are praying for blessing, you are longing to see your church revived. Brother ministers [and members] has God handled the last piece? Many pieces have been handled, and I believe that there are men and women God has been handling; this piece has gone on the altar and that piece has not yet been handled. Let us be honest, let us be realistic. I believe we are not going to see the movement we long for, and streams from the river of God, until Christian men and women cry out to God, 'Oh handle the last piece.' If the fire is to fall the last piece must be handled. The truth about the Holy Spirit is discoverable and verifiable only by submission to His power. We may talk about Him, we may think about Him, but only when we submit can we know His mighty power.[2]

William Williams, called the 'sweet singer of Wales', put in just one short verse his relationship with their Saviour, thus:

> Jesus, Jesus, All-Sufficient,
> beyond telling is your worth,
> in your name lie greater treasures
> than the richest found on earth,
> Such abundance
> is my portion with my God.

Poetic words perhaps, but for our heroes they expressed a reality they could not deny or keep to themselves. Like the prophet Daniel, they would not compromise under the most severe circumstances.

While researching for this book I came across a little volume which hadn't been borrowed from the library for over a decade. I quote from the *Power of Pentecost* by the Reverend Thomas Waugh. Although written eighty years ago, it could have been written today:

How are we to account for the fearful gap between our Christian activities and practical results? How is it that with such a host of noble toilers, and such vast resources at our disposal, the outcome is so bitterly disappointing? We affirm that the true answer is this: *The Church of God is not to-day as she was at the beginning, 'filled with the Holy Ghost.'* This baptism is our great need, underlying all our other needs, and until that is met we shall have no general revival of the work of God on a great scale.

Our danger is to rely upon men, methods [modern technology], and money, instead of relying upon Him who alone can raise up the men and equip them, suggest the methods and vitalize them, bring in the money and make it a blessing when we have got it. . . . Certainly we want more men of the highest possible gifts and human qualifications, but still more urgent is our need of more of the power of God. Whatever the men [and women], whatever their gifts, whatever our legislation and methods, and whatever the temporal wealth of the Church, <u>it is all so much dead machinery, unless it be vitalized and made effective by the mighty power of the Spirit of Pentecost.</u>

The activities of the Church to-day are wonderful, and we cannot be too grateful for them; yet how heart-breaking is our progress! The reason is that, with all our activities, the spiritual tone of the Church is low, the temperature is terribly down. There is not heat enough to ripen the fruit. The only heat that can ripen fruit for God's garner is the fire of Pentecost. That fire comes upon the Churches in answer to prayer, and too many churches have almost given up praying. Thank God, many churches pray more than ever, and many individual Christians too. Nevertheless, a number of churches have lost their love for, and their confidence in, what our forefathers understood by united prayer. . . . And yet the Christian Church was born in a prayer-meeting; it was upon pleading men and women that the mighty chrism [holy oil] of the Spirit first fell.

Dr Martyn Lloyd-Jones, in his sermons on revival, considers the story of when the disciples of Christ returned to Him bitterly complaining that they could not cast out one particular demon. Jesus replied, "This kind can come forth by nothing but by prayer and fasting" (Mark 9:28–29).

> In other words, what Our Lord is saying to the disciples can be put like this. He said, in effect, 'You have failed in this particular case because the power that you had and which was sufficient and adequate for other cases, is inadequate and has no value here. It just leaves you utterly helpless and it leaves the boy in his diseased and powerless condition. . . . You will never be able to deal with 'this kind' unless you have applied to God for the power which he alone can give you. You must realise that you are confronted by something that is too deep for your methods to get rid of, or to deal with, and you need something that can go down beneath the evil power, shatter it, and there is only one thing that can do that, and that is the power of God. And we, too, must become aware of that, we have got to feel it until we become desperate. We must ask ourselves how we can succeed if we do not have this authority, this commission, this might and strength and power. We must become utterly and absolutely convinced of our need. We must cease to have so much confidence in ourselves, and in all our methods and organisations, and in our slickness. We have got to realise that we must be filled with God's Spirit.[3]

When speaking of revival we have often heard people say, "Today things are different. It could never happen today." Has God changed? Has His Word changed? Has God's power diminished or His love abated? Of course not. It is only because we limit His power in our minds that we convince ourselves He is not up to the task of a dramatic change, and that He will not move so powerfully today. Some who have never heard about true Holy Spirit revival think that the low number of converts is the norm, and they believe what they read in the Book of Acts was just for the Early Church; never was anything further from the truth.

God is sovereign in the affairs of His kingdom and yet He must long for us to want Him to revive His Church, the Bride of Christ, in our day. Revival starts with us in the Church. The Reverend

Duncan Campbell often used to say, "God is looking for the man He can trust with revival."

The last words of this book are from Holy Scripture and were penned under divine inspiration by the apostle Paul. The apostle had seen and experienced the dynamic power of the risen Christ in his life and in the lives of the new Christians in the communities that he visited. In his letter he asks God to give the Ephesian Christians the 'Spirit of wisdom and revelation'. Then he also prays that

> the eyes of their hearts may be enlightened regarding God's power . . . that you may know the hope to which He has called you, the riches of his glorious inheritance in the saints, and *His incomparably great power for us who believe.* That power is like the working of His mighty strength, which he exerted in Christ when He raised Him from the dead and seated Him at His right hand in the heavenly realms, far above all rule and authority, power and dominion, and every title that can be given, not only in the present age but also in the one to come [Ephesians 1:18–21].

### Prayer:

Almighty God, in Christ you make all things new:
transform the poverty of our nature by the riches of your grace,
and in the renewal of our lives make known your heavenly glory;
through Jesus Christ our Lord. Amen.[4]

**Notes:**

1. *The Lord's Supper*, Evangelical Press, London, 1966.

2. *The Price and Power of Revival: Lessons from the Hebrides Awakening* by the Reverend Duncan Campbell, Faith Mission, Edinburgh (no date).

3. *Revival: Can We Make It Happen?* by Martyn Lloyd-Jones, Marshal Pickering, Basingstoke, 1986.

4. The collect for the second Sunday after Epiphany, Common Worship.

*Portrait of Thomas Charles.*

*Statue of Thomas Charles at Bala.*

*St Mary Magdalene Church, Sparkford, Somerset.*

*St Mary Magdalene Church, Sparkford, interior.*

*St Mary Magdalene Church, Sparkford, Somerset.*

*St Barnabas Church, Queen Camel, Somerset.*

*Thomas and Sally Charles's shop and home, Bala.*

*Swan Stairs, City of London.*

*Memorial Plaque to John Morgan at Newport, Pembrokeshire.*

# APPENDIX 1

# THE MONUMENT TO GRIFFITH JONES ERECTED BY MADAM BEVAN IN THE CHURCH AT LLANDDOWROR, CARMARTHENSHIRE

SACRED TO THE MEMORY
OF THE REVEREND MR. GRIFFITH JONES.
Rector of this Parish and of Llandilo:
He was presented to the latter, July 3, 1711,
To the former, July 27, 1716.
From his first admission into holy orders
He devoted himself wholly to the duties
Of his sacred function;
Which he continued faithfully and conscientiously
To discharge throughout the course
Of a long life:
Conscious of the importance of the vocation therewith he was called,
He applied all his time and attention
To that one great concern which came upon him daily,
"The care of the Churches:"
In his preaching
He inculcated the plainest and most obvious duties of Christianity;
Which he enforced upon the minds of his hearers
With a truly Christian zeal,
And in so interesting a manner that none could depart
Unaffected or unedified.
Nor was he an instructor from the pulpit only;
His own example added weight to every precept,
His whole life was a constant illustration of
The religion which he taught:

The circulating Welsh Charity Schools
Owe their rise, progress and continuance, to his
Humane and beneficent disposition;
This pious undertaking was attended with such success,
Under his management and conduct,
That at the time of his decease,
The number of schools exceeded three thousand; of scholars,
An hundred and fifty-eight thousand:
He was indefatigable and successful likewise
In procuring two large impressions of the Welsh Bible,
Which were sold at a low price for the
Benefit of the poor:
He composed and published several useful books
On religious subjects, in Welsh and English;
He sought out all opportunities of doing good;
It was the business of his life to approve himself on all occasions
The vigilant and faithful pastor,
The sincere and devout Christian,
The good man:
Though placed in an inferior station in the church,
He performed services in the cause of religion
Which would have reflected a lustre
On the highest:
The divine Providence,
Which had lent him long as a blessing to his country,
Was pleased to remove him,
On the eighth day of April, 1761,
In the seventy-eighth year of his age
To an eternity of happiness in heaven
Where his conversation had always been.

Monument was erected by a Person, desirous of paying every
mark of regard to such distinguished merit.

# APPENDIX 2

# PLACES TO EXPLORE MENTIONED IN THIS BOOK

**Wales:**

- Statue of Thomas Charles, Bala, Merioneth
- Mary Jones World, St Beuno's Church, Llanycil, Bala. (The Bible Society).
- Mary Jones Memorial, Llanfihangel-y-pennant, Merioneth.
- Portrait of Madam Bevan, Carmarthenshire County Museum, Abergwili, Carmarthen.
- Parish Church, Llanddowror, Carmarthenshire.
- Laugharne, Carmarthenshire.
- Picton Castle, near Narberth, Pembrokeshire.
- Memorial to Sir John Philipps, St Mary's Church, Haverfordwest.
- Gwynfil Chapel, Llangeitho, Ceredigion.
- Statue of Daniel Rowland, Llangeitho, Ceredigion.
- St Ceitho Parish Church, Llangeitho, Ceredigion.
- Parish Church, Llandewi-Brefi, Ceredigion.
- Parish Church, Talgarth, Powys.
- Trevecka College, Trefecca, Powys.
- Museum of Welsh Life, St Fagans, Cardiff (see the Thomas Charles Sunday-school bronze medal).
- University of Wales Library, Aberystwyth.

**England:**

- St Barnabas Church, Queen Camel, Somerset.
- St John the Evangelist, Milborne Port, Somerset.
- St Mary Magdalene, Sparkford, Somerset.
- St Michael's, Shepton Beauchamp, Somerset.
- Swan Stairs (Swan Lane), London Bridge, London.

# BIBLIOGRAPHY

William Hughes. *Life and Letters of the Rev. Thomas Charles, B.A., of Bala*, J. Morris, Rhyl, 1881.

J. Davies, *Three Sermons by the Rev. Mr. Daniel Rowland* (translated from Welsh), London, 1778.

Joseph Evans of Denbigh, *Biographical Dictionary of Ministers and Preachers of the Welsh Calvinist Methodist Body or Presbyterians of Wales*, D. O'Brien Owen, CM Book Agency, Carnarvon, 1907.

D. E. Jenkins, *The Life of the Rev. Thomas Charles, B.A., of Bala* (limited edition in three volumes; total of 1,925 pages), Llewelyn Jenkins, Denbigh, 1908.

David Jones, *The Life and Times of Griffith Jones Sometime Rector of Llanddowror*, SPCK, 1902.

Griffith Jones, *Sermons*, Volume 1, Evangelical Library (Cat B4.3), London.

Edward Morgan, *Ministerial Records or Brief Accounts of the Great Progress of Religion*, H. Hughes, London, 1840.

Edward Morgan, *Essays, Letters and Interesting Papers of the Rev. Thomas Charles, B.A., of Bala*. R. B. Seeley and W. Burnside, London, 1836.

Edward Morgan (editor), *Letters of Griffith Jones to Mrs. Bevan, 1723–8*, Whittaker & Co. and Seely & Co., London, 1832.

J. Morison, *The Fathers and Founders of the London Missionary Society*, Fisher, Son & Co., London (no date).

John Owen, *Sermons by the Reverend Griffith Jones*, Hamilton, Adams & Co., circa 1832.

Daniel Rowland. *13 Sermons* (translated from Welsh), Briggs, Hull, 1788.

Daniel Rowland, *3 Sermons* (translated from Welsh by the Reverend John Davies, 1778), ECCO Print Editions (no date).

L. Tyerman, *The Life of the Rev. George Whitefield*, Hodder & Stoughton, 1876.

William Williams of Crickhowell, *Welsh Calvinistic Methodism*,

James Nisbet & Co., London, 1872. (Third edition enlarged, Bryntirion Press, Bridgend, 1998).

David Young, *The Origin and History of Methodism in Wales and the Borders*, Charles H. Kelly, London, 1893.

M. Philipps, *The History of the Family of Philipps of Picton*, London, 1906.

R. Bennett, *The Early Life of Howell Harris*, The Banner of Truth Trust, London, 1962.

F. A. Cavenagh, *The Life and Work of Griffith Jones of Llanddowror*, University of Wales PB, 1930.

G. Davies, *Trevecka, 1706–1964*, Volume XV, the Brecknock Society in Brycheiniog, 1971 (reprinted by Colin Richards, 2001).

B. H. Edwards, *Revival: A People Saturated with God.* Evangelical Press, Darlington, 1990.

Gwyn Davies, *A Light in the Land: Christianity in Wales, 200–2000*, Bryntirion Press, 2002.

E. Evans, *Daniel Rowland and the Great Evangelical Awakening in Wales*, The Banner of Truth Trust, Edinburgh, 1985.

E. Evans, *Bread of Heaven: The Life and Work of William Williams*, *Pantycelyn*, Bryntirion Press, Bridgend, 2011.

Geraint H. Jenkins, *Literature Religion and Society in Wales, 1660–1730.* University of Wales, 1978.

*Picton Castle and Grounds* (introduction by Susan Philipps), Hudsons Media, Peterborough, 2012.

Hero von Friesen and Thomas Lloyd, *The Families of Picton*, Picton Castle Trust, Picton, 2002.

Owen Thomas, *The Atonement Controversy*, The Banner of Truth Trust, Edinburgh, 2002.

Christopher J. Tokeley, 'Remembering Daniel Rowland', *In Writing*, No. 110, Evangelical Library. London.

Christopher J. Tokeley, 'Griffith Jones of Llanddowror', *In Writing*, No. 114, Evangelical Library, London.

G. Tudur, *Howell Harris from Conversion to Separation, 1735–1750*, University of Wales, Cardiff, 2000.

Thomas Waugh, *The Power of Pentecost*, Thomas Champness, Rochdale, 1935.

# TIMELINE OF GRIFFITH JONES

| 1684 | Born at Pant-yr-fel, Pemboyr, Carmarthenshire. |
|------|-----|
| 1684 | Baptised at Cilrhedyn. |
| 1708 | Ordained by Bishop Bull; appointed curate at Penbryn, Cardiganshire. |
| 1709 | Appointed curate at Laugharne, Carmarthenshire. |
| 1711 | Appointed Rector of Llandeilo-Abercowyn, Carmarthenshire. |
| 1713 | Prepares for service in India. |
| 1714 | Brought before Bishop Ottley on charges. |
| 1716 | Appointed Rector of Llanddowror by Sir John Philipps. |
| 1717 | Supports new edition of Welsh Bible. |
| 1718 | Undertakes preaching tour of Scotland. |
| 1720 | Marries Margaret Philipps. |
| 1731 | Corresponds with the SPCK regarding Welsh schools. |
| 1727 | Supports new edition of the Welsh Bible. |
| 1734/5 | Daniel Rowland converted through Jones' message. |
| 1737 | Schools in Wales have 2,400 scholars; death of Sir John Philipps. |
| 1755 | Death of Margaret, Jones' wife. |
| 1761 | Jones' death, leaving a legacy of 3,495 schools and 158,000 pupils. |

# TIMELINE OF DANIEL ROWLAND

| 1713 | Born to the Reverend Daniel and Jannet Rowland. |
|------|-----|
| 1733 | Ordained deacon in London. |
| 1734 | Marries Eleanor Davies of Caerlllugest. |
| 1734/5 | Converted through Griffith Jones at Llandewi-Brefi. |
| 1735 | Son John born to Rowland and Eleanor. |
| 1737 | Meets Howell Harris. |

| 1760 | Brother drowned; Daniel's son succeeds his uncle at Llangeitho. |
|------|---|
| 1762 | Revival sweeps Llangeitho and the surrounding area. |
| 1763 | Ejected from the Church of England. |
| 1769 | Offered living at Newport, Pembrokeshire. |
| 1773 | Thomas Charles converted at Llangeitho. |
| 1790 | Dies at Llangeitho, aged seventy-seven. |

## TIMELINE OF THOMAS CHARLES

| 1753 | Sally Jones born. |
|------|---|
| 1755 | Thomas born to Rees and Jael Charles at Longmoor Farm, Carmarthenshire. |
| 1763 | Attends Griffith Jones' school at Llanddowror. |
| 1769 | Attends Carmarthen Academy. |
| 1773 | Converted through hearing Daniel Rowland at Llangeitho. |
| 1775 | Becomes an undergraduate at Jesus College, Oxford. |
| 1778 | Ordained to curacies in Somerset. |
| 1779 | In autumn Thomas writes his first letter to Sally Jones. |
| 1783 | In summer resigns curacy at Sparkford, Somerset. |
| 1783 | Marries Sally Jones at Llanycil, Bala. |
| 1783–4 | Curacies cut short in Wales owing to his evangelical views. |
| 1784 | Enrolled as member of the Methodist Society, Bala. |
| 1804 | Bible Society established due to efforts of Thomas Charles. |
| 1814 | Dies at Bala. |